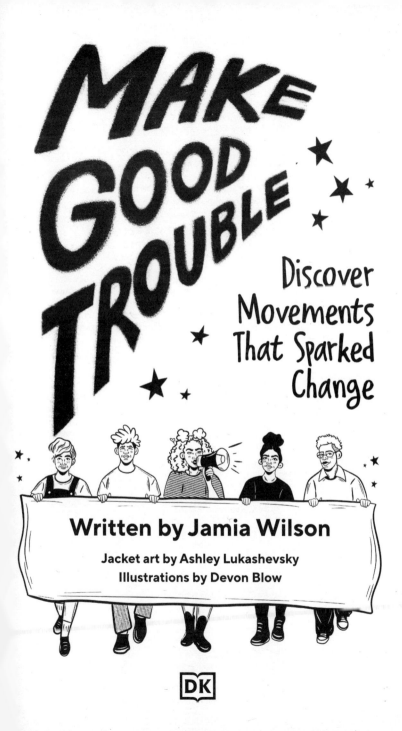

MAKE GOOD TROUBLE

Discover Movements That Sparked Change

Written by Jamia Wilson

Jacket art by Ashley Lukashevsky
Illustrations by Devon Blow

DK

First American Edition, 2025
Published in the United States by DK Publishing,
a division of Penguin Random House LLC
1745 Broadway, 20th Floor, New York, NY 10019

25 26 27 28 29 10 9 8 7 6 5 4 3 2 1
001–334614–Feb/2025

Published in Great Britain by Dorling Kindersley Limited

A catalog record for this book
is available from the Library of Congress.

ISBN 978-0-7440-9219-6

DK books are available at special discounts when purchased in bulk
for sales promotions, premiums, fund-raising, or educational use.

For details, contact: DK Publishing Special Markets,
1745 Broadway, 20th Floor, New York, NY 10019
SpecialSales@dk.com

Printed and bound in Great Britain

www.dk.com

MIX
Paper | Supporting
responsible forestry
FSC™ C018179

This book was made with Forest
Stewardship Council™ certified
paper—one small step in DK's
commitment to a sustainable future.
Learn more at www.dk.com/uk/
information/sustainability

Dedicated to the cycle breakers
who journey toward freedom with open hearts
and expansive dreams.

To Martin "Marty" Stuart Swist.
Thank you for shaping the future by seeing,
inspiring, and supporting young readers worldwide.
I hope we will continue to make you proud as you
run the big library of the great beyond.
I promise we will continue to "make good trouble."

A note from the Publisher

CONTENTS

"BE REALISTIC; DEMAND THE IMPOSSIBLE."

FRENCH STUDENTS, PARIS 1968

"One child, one teacher, one book, one pen can change the world."
MALALA YOUSAFZAI

"It's up to all of us—Black, white, everyone."
MICHELLE OBAMA

PEOPLE HAVE POWER!

INTRODUCTION

On April 25, 2004, I stood amid a vast crowd as a young campus organizer in the monumental *March For Women's Lives* in Washington, DC. At the forefront of **1.15 million marchers**, I carried the introductory banner alongside fellow activists from across the United States, representing recent graduates and students from high schools and college campuses nationwide.

Before the march, as the sun began to rise, a revered elder arrived and demanded that we yield our place at the front for more distinguished elder stateswomen and celebrities. Despite my stomach flopping as if it would fly through my throat, a mantra echoed within:

"I am the future. We are the future."

Feet firmly planted, memories flooded my mind—of my mother's tales, recounting investigative journalist *Ida B. Wells*'s defiance in the face of segregation during a pivotal suffragist march. Like Ida, we refused to retreat to the rear.

My mother's words fueled my resolve, as did feminist writer and activist *Gloria Steinem*'s wisdom: **"When children say, 'It's not fair,' and, 'You are not the boss of me,' they already have the core of every social justice movement."** I was still floating on air after Gloria's inspiring pep talk to a group of organizers in the weeks before our march. **We were heirs to a legacy of defiance.**

While honoring those who came before, **we recognized our role in shaping the future.** Although the elder who asked us to move was upset in that moment, the reality was that we were following her lead and taking our opportunity to make our mark. We learned that day that change happens when we **carry the torch together** instead of waiting to have it passed our way.

Linked arm in arm, we marched forward, eyes fixed on a world of justice and equality, heads held high.

Shortly before her passing, my mother, *Freda*, shared her heartfelt wish for me to work with others to **continue bettering the world.** Reflecting on her trailblazing work in civil rights and disability justice that started in her teens, she urged,

"Get on up and keep it moving."

With her loving smile and a gentle squeeze of my hand, she emphasized the importance of our ongoing efforts, affirming that **each generation builds upon the last** until we all achieve freedom. She said,

"Even if people who don't get it question you or make you feel like you don't know, you do know the way forward. You hear me? You do know."

And now, I'm here, writing this book in honor of her many lessons, including how to sit in, march, sing protest songs, and other forms of nonviolent civil disobedience.

I believe what **"you do know"** will help us find our way toward justice and liberation.

In the spirit of the changemakers in this book, I ask you to take your rightful place on the page of the present and on into the future, using the compass of your conscience, heart, and mind to lead us forward. There's much to heal and change, and the stakes are high.

Let's keep it moving.

WHY MOVEMENTS MATTER

 In the following pages, I invite you to join me on a journey through the ages where young people dare shape <u>a more just and freer world.</u>

Coretta Scott King—a tireless advocate for civil rights, nuclear peace, an end to apartheid, LGBTQIA+ rights, and the legislative and cultural movement to establish *Martin Luther King Jr. Day* in the United States—once declared, **"Struggle is a never-ending process. Freedom is never really won; you earn it and win it in every generation."** The young changemakers you will meet in these stories personify this truth, **creating and fueling movements that echo across time**.

We'll return to a pivotal moment just before the turn of the 20th century, when the *Newsies*, mostly children and teens, took to the New York City streets to protest unfair treatment by newspaper moguls. Their fierce spirit and unity in the face of cruelty led to the *Newsboys' Strike* of 1899—a powerful testament to the enduring impact of <u>collective action,</u> even in our modern world. Though a century old, this event resonates with the youth-led protests demanding urgent environmental action from Sweden to the Philippines—showing that the **power of youth activism** transcends time and borders.

Amid the clattering looms of Lowell, Massachusetts, we'll witness the *Lowell Mill Workers Movement*. These were not just "factory girls," but young individuals who dared to defy the brutal working conditions in textile mills. Their **organizing** and solidarity, driven by their courage and resilience, made way for reforms and helped shift culture. We'll meet legendary Civil Rights Movement leader and politician *John Lewis*, who urged people to **make "good trouble"** to create social change. Lewis was known as the *"Conscience of the Congress"* due to his moral integrity as a policymaker. His words sparked a fire within the hearts of young activists, inspiring a lasting legacy of action.

MAKE GOOD TROUBLE

We'll learn about the landmark case, *Tinker* v. *Des Moines*, where *Mary Beth Tinker*, alongside her siblings and peers, etched her name In history by wearing a black armband to protest peacefully against the Vietnam War. Their landmark Supreme Court case **solidified the rights of students to express themselves**, marking a triumph for youth activism that is still important to student advocates taking a stand today.

And we'll zoom in on the present, where the *Extinction Rebellion Youth* is rising as a global clarion call to combat climate change and protect our planet for future generations. Young activists are **uniting millions of people** to fight for a sustainable future, showing that the power of youth activism transcends borders and unites us all.

Although the youth you'll encounter throughout *Make Good Trouble* may use different tools, lead their own movements or join with others, speak different languages, and live in various cultures, they all forge pathways toward a more just and equitable world. Their approaches to activism may be different, but they all show how taking a stand for **what we believe in and care about can unite us** in our drive to make the world better for ourselves and for those who come next.

LOWELL MILL FACTORY GIRLS REVOLT

> "Oh! Isn't it a pity, such a pretty girl as I should be sent to the factory to pine away and die? ... I will not be a slave, for I'm so fond of liberty ..."

the *Lowell Mill* textile factory workers sang in time to the factory bells.

In the 1830s and 1840s, few laws protected laborers, including children, who endured harsh working conditions. On average, the *"mill girls,"* as they were known, **worked 12 to 14 hours daily**, with a half-day on Saturdays and only Sundays off. They toiled for 10 months a year outside of three holidays. Nicknamed *"operatives"* because of their spinning machines, they had to attend church regularly and follow strict rules. Workers often **shared rooms with up to seven people** and even shared beds.

An 11-year-old doffer, *Harriet Hanson Robinson*, watched as her older coworker delivered **the first public speech by a woman** in Lowell, Massachusetts, urging peers to resist wage cuts.

This became a **turning point** for their community, the textile industry, and labor rights.

To define their ideals, they organized the *Lowell Factory Girls Association*, wrote their own constitution, and held **"turnout"** strikes in 1834 and 1836. Seeking independence, education, and exposure outside the home, the mill girls united when **owners cut wages by 15%**, increased the work pace, and raised the rent for factory housing. From 1840 to 1845, they published the *Lowell Offering*, a magazine featuring their poetry, essays, and fiction.

Despite being attacked as **"ungrateful and unwomanly"** and **"Amazons,"** the workers pushed for 10-hour shifts, condemned pay cuts, and declared, **"union is power."** Although their initial demands were not met after about 800 strikers marched, their efforts laid the groundwork for ongoing collective action.

"UNION IS POWER"

The movement continued for years with **petitions and other tactics**, strengthening over time. In 1845, the Lowell factory girls founded the *Lowell Female Labor Reform Association*, lobbying the state legislature for a shortened workday, building on what the earlier strikers had started.

Today, the mill girls' legacy endures in the suffragist, anti-slavery, free speech, and labor movements. Their vision and courage inspired the **first union of working women and girls** in the United States, paving the way for later labor uprisings.

CARLISLE CHILDREN STAND STRONG AGAINST INJUSTICE

In 1879, under the dark cover of an October night, 82 Brule Sioux and Oglala Sioux children from the occupied Dakota Territory arrived at the *Carlisle Indian School* in Pennsylvania. Led by Civil War veteran *Richard Henry Pratt* and interpreter *Luther Standing Bear*, the children were taken to a barren former military barracks with no food or bedding, their moccasins stripped, and their long braids cut, **severing ties to their cultural identity**.

> Children ... were punished for speaking their languages and forced to march in formation.

Three years after *Sitting Bull*'s victory over *General Custer*, Pratt, a Baptist with the motto "Kill the Indian in him, and save the man," sought to **"civilize"** Indigenous children by immersing them in European-American customs and religion. Carlisle became the model for many such schools aimed at **erasing Indigenous culture**. For over a century, hundreds of these schools subjected children to forced labor, disease, and severe punishments, **resulting in over 500 deaths**.

Life at Carlisle was harsh. Children from more than 140 diverse groups were **punished for speaking their languages** and forced to march in formation. Boys learned trades like blacksmithing and carpentry, while girls were taught laundry, sewing, and baking. **Spiritual ceremonies and using given names were forbidden**, leading to severe punishments for those who resisted.

Students rebelled against the <u>harsh conditions</u> by running away, using Indigenous Plains Sign Talk, and secretly learning each other's languages. They documented their stories through Native graphic art on chalkboards. These **acts of defiance forged connections** that inspired future movements like the *American Indian Movement* and the *Standing Rock Protest.*

Secretary of the Interior Deb Haaland, the first Native American US cabinet secretary, announced a *Federal Indian Boarding School Initiative* in 2021. The initiative is working to fix the long-lasting damage caused by these schools with a formal apology, support for those affected, a memorial, educating the public, and more. The fight for **accountability, cultural preservation, and the restoration of occupied lands** continues today.

NEWSIES' STRIKE: THE FIGHT FOR FAIR WAGES

"Extra! Extra! Read all about it!" shouted the newsies. Newsies were often immigrant, homeless, and orphaned children who bought newspapers at a wholesale price and sold them on New York City's street corners for pennies. At the end of the 19th century, **the public depended on daily newspapers as their primary news source**. Newsies hawked papers after school, buying bundles of papers at 50 cents per 100 that they sold for 1 cent each.

Between 1898 and 1899, newspaper sales and the competition between *William Randolph Hearst* and *Joseph Pulitzer,* the wealthy *Journal* and *New York World* owners, climbed sharply. Many newspapers **took advantage of tragedies by focusing on exaggeration** (similar to some fake news stories today) to boost sales.

"EXTRA! EXTRA! READ ALL ABOUT IT!"

Hearst and Pulitzer **cashed in on crises** such as the *Spanish–American War* and <u>raised their wholesale rate</u> from five to six cents. The newsies felt the pinch from the price increase and **suffered from hunger and exhaustion** while working long hours for about **only 26 cents per day**. Outraged by the moguls' inflated bundle charges and dismissal of their complaints, newsies aged 7 and up **demanded fair wages**.

"Just stick together and we'll win,"

said *Louis Balletti,* nicknamed *Kid Blink*. Blink was an Italian American 18-year-old newsie known for his red hair, eye patch, and **voice as a strike spokesperson**. He declared,

> "I'm trying to figure out how 10 cents on 100 papers can mean more to a millionaire than it does to newsboys, and I can't see it."

By marching, holding rallies, and speaking publicly about their plight, the newsies' might **forced the owners to negotiate**. The newsies <u>organized massive protests</u>, rallying thousands of supporters. They stopped delivering papers, **causing a significant drop in sales** for Hearst and Pulitzer. The public supported the newsies, boycotting the newspapers.

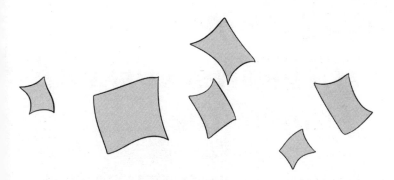

In August of 1899, the <u>owners struck a deal</u> with the newsies. The **publishers agreed to buy back unsold papers**, ensuring the newsies wouldn't lose money on bundles they couldn't sell. This victory was a significant step forward, showcasing the

power of unity in labor organizing.

WRZEŚNIA CHILDREN'S CULTURAL REVOLUTION

Tekla Tomaszewska fainted. It was late May in 1901, and the shoemaker's daughter from Września, a west-central Polish town seized by Prussia, had just **returned from** *Catholic People's School* (Katolicka Szkoła Ludowa) **with bloodied hands.**

Since 1878, Poles living in territories impacted by the *Prussian Partition* were pushed to **conform to widespread Germanization policies**. These policies were put in place to spread the German language through **"Kulturkampf,"** or culture struggle. Prussian authorities assumed that forcing Polish students to speak German would **create devoted subjects,** but their <u>efforts backfired.</u>

The strike expanded across Poland for four years and eroded Prussian authorities' attempts to stamp out Polish identity.

Students were struck with lashes on their backsides and palms, but they resisted their teachers' demands by **refusing to respond in German**. The Prussian teachers' blows were so harsh that the pupils could not hold their books in their inflamed hands. Parents were pushed to enter the school after hearing their cries. As more citizens resisted, they were **arrested and charged**. The Prussian court slammed the parents with a conviction in a bid to **stop the rebellion**.

In May 1901, Tekla's father, *Andrzej*, gathered with other parents to object to the confinement of their children, who were held after school for refusing to speak, sing, or pray in German during religion class. Religion was the sole and final subject taught in Polish under occupation, stirring **14 courageous students**, including Tekla, **to rise up with a strike.**

The strike **expanded across Poland** for six years and eroded Prussian authorities' attempts to **stamp out Polish identity**. The heroism of the Września community captured the attention of artists, scholars, writers, and a *Nobel Prize* winner, *Henryk Sienkiewicz*, whose advocacy amplified their cause worldwide. Today, the Wrześnian children are still celebrated as an example of **young people's important role as leaders in the fight for freedom.**

MOTHER JONES AND THE MARCH OF THE MILL CHILDREN

In 1902, *Mary Harris Jones*, a silver-haired, bonnet-wearing, 5-foot-tall immigrant widow of 66, was called

"the most dangerous woman in America."

She may have been described by the press as looking like a sweet grandmother, but Mary, also known as *"Mother Jones,"* was a fierce fighter against <u>unfair labor practices</u> from the late 1800s through the 1920s. Factory and mine owners were scared of her ability to convince workers in all sorts of industries—mining, textiles, steel—to put down their tools and **strike until they got better pay and working conditions**.

Mary's journey as an activist began in the 1880s, when she saw the **harsh poverty** outside her Chicago dress-shop window and compared it to the fancy lives of wealthy bosses who didn't seem to care. She became famous for speaking out for child workers at a time when **at least one in six American children under 16 had to work**. Mary knew all about tough childhoods. Her grandfather was hanged for standing up to British troops during the <u>Irish potato famine</u>, and her dad had to escape to America. In 1842, Mary and her family sailed first to Canada and then to the United States.

A time when at least one in six American children under 16 had to work.

In 1903, Mother Jones **organized around 200 workers**, including children, **to march almost 100 miles** from Philadelphia to New York. They wanted everyone to know about the **terrible working conditions** children faced. They demanded shorter work weeks, with young mill workers carrying signs like, "We Want Time to Play" and "We Want to Go to School."

Their three-week march ended at *President Roosevelt's summer home* in Long Island, but he refused to meet them. Even so, the bravery of Mother Jones and the young activists helped **create laws to protect child workers** and made people more aware of the problem.

YOUNG FILIPINA FEMINISTS LEAD THE WAY

"What a man can do, a woman can do just as well."

Two years before she was crowned in 1908, 22-year-old beauty queen and mestiza journalist *Pura Villanueva Kalaw* helped organize the feminist group the *Asociacion Feminista Ilonga*. Guided by their motto, "What a man can do, a woman can do just as well," Kalaw's group partnered with the *Asociacion Feminista Filipina*, who had formed the <u>first women-led</u> suffrage movement in the Philippines. A year before, *Paz Natividad vda. de Zulueta* had started the movement from her home in Manila **to advocate for social aid and women's civic participation at a time when politicians were mostly male.**

Although women from the Philippines served as guerrillas, fundraisers, storytellers, and front-line nurses in the **fight for self-rule** during the *Philippine–American War* (1899-1902), in the years that followed, they still **battled barriers to equality** in health care, access to clean milk for children, education, safety, labor rights, and the right to vote. *Clemencia López, María de Villamor, María Arévalo, Helen Wilson, Felix de Calderon, Trinidad Rizal, Bonifacia Delgado de Barretto*, and other determined women gathered and traveled the country to build support.

The **seeds planted by the founding mothers of Filipina feminism** bloomed into a far-reaching history of women's participation in positions of power after the **country's first suffrage bill** made it to the government. It was later passed into law in 1937, giving Filipinas access to the ballot. Their leadership also paved the way for more access to health care in response to troubling infant and maternal death rates in poor communities.

While attempts to **advance equality** continue, the fruits of the Asociacion Feminista Filipina's work endure as the country ranks in the **top 10 most gender-equal states** in East Asia and the Pacific. In 1973, eight years before the United States confirmed its

first woman Supreme Court Justice *Cecilia Muñoz Palma* served on the Philippines' highest court. As of 2023, 59 of the 193 *United Nations* member states have had just one female leader, but **two Filipinas have served as president in the past half-century.**

BESSIE WATSON'S BOLD FIGHT FOR VOTING RIGHTS

"VOTES FOR WOMEN"

read the bold words on a purple, green, and white sash worn by 9-year-old *Elizabeth "Bessie" Watson*. Bessie was proudly wearing her sash as she **marched for women's suffrage** at an event that also saw *Emmeline Pankhurst*, the leader of the British suffrage movement then known by many as "suffragettes," speak to the crowd of hundreds.

When Bessie and her mother had spotted an advertisement for a pageant featuring historic Scottish women organized by the *Women's Social and Political Union* (WSPU), Bessie was inspired by the WSPU's promise to showcase **"what women have done and can do."** For Bessie, that meant playing her bagpipes.

It had been two years earlier, in 1907, when 7-year-old Bessie first learned to play the bagpipes. Her aunt had **died of tuberculosis** in Bessie's home, and Bessie had been urged to play the pipes to fortify her lungs and prevent illness. Born in Edinburgh, Scotland, Bessie was a frail child and played a

half-sized set of pipes to fit her small stature. Girl pipers were rare at the time, and it was **unusual for any child her age to play** this grand woodwind instrument, whose earliest usage was to motivate troops and frighten rival armies on the front lines of war.

Bessie was inspired by the WSPU's promise to showcase "what women have done and can do."

Despite her young age and the fact that she was **not yet old enough to vote**, Bessie fearlessly left her mark on the history of women's suffrage. After her school hours, she would rush

to *Calton Jail*, where her fellow **suffragists were imprisoned and force-fed** during their hunger strikes. With her hair adorned with ribbons in the **suffrage colors of purple, green, and white**, she would play her pipes outside the prison walls, not only to uplift her comrades, but also **to draw attention to their cause**.

VOTES FOR WOMEN

Small but mighty, Bessie brought the WSPU's motto, **"deeds not words,"** to life with her plucky dedication.

DEEDS NOT WORDS

In 1918, voting rights were granted to women over 30 with higher incomes, class positions, and property ownership, but it wasn't until 1928 that the WSPU and their comrades' hard-fought battle paid off, when all women over 21 in England, Wales, and Scotland **won the right to vote on equal terms with men.**

THE SHIRTWAIST STRIKE

"I'm a working girl," declared *Clara Lemlich*, speaking in Yiddish to the crowd of overworked laborers at a large union gathering in New York City. "I am one of those who suffer from abuses, and I move that we go on a general strike." Clara had already been **arrested over a dozen times for her activism** and was suffering from broken ribs from cruel factory guards.

Six years earlier, in 1903, the 23-year-old strike leader had emigrated from Horodok, Ukraine, after a pogrom in nearby Kishinev. Like many young immigrant workers striving to make a living, Clara now toiled for long hours as a garment laborer in a crowded, dirty, and unsafe environment for about $6 per week.

When asked to take an oath of loyalty to the action, Clara said,

"If I turn traitor to the cause I now pledge, may my hand wither from the arm I now raise."

As the crowd also raised their arms in unity, **the largest uprising ever staged by women workers to date** was born. Around 20,000 of the 32,000 New York City workers making shirtwaists—a practical button-up blouse often worn with long skirts and associated with independent working women—<u>refused to work</u> in the following days, demanding a higher wage, safer conditions, and a shorter work week.

After experiencing brutality caused by attackers hired by the factory owners and bribed police officers, **the women went without pay**, struggling to feed their families but never giving in.

When the strike ended in 1910, workers received better pay and could work fewer hours. However, the factory owners still **refused to address safety issues**, including faulty fire escapes. Tragically, when a fire broke out in 1911 in the *Triangle Shirtwaist Factory*, 146 workers died, including 123 women and teenage girls. The rapid spread of the inferno was made worse because there was only one fire escape, and doors were locked shut by **biased factory management** who were suspicious of theft and wanted to limit employee breaks.

The disaster **caused outrage** and showed the public the urgent need for better workplace safety measures. It sped up the growth of the *International Ladies' Garment Workers' Union*, which fought against sweatshops for almost a century. Clara Lemlich's <u>courage and leadership</u> in the Shirtwaist Strike helped set the stage for these **crucial reforms.**

THE SCOUTING MOVEMENT

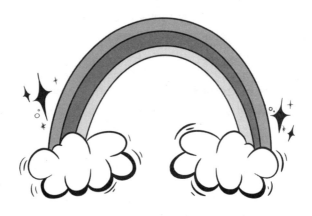

The Scouting Movement began with a group camping trip on Brownsea Island, UK, in 1907 with 20 boys attending. A book followed in 1908, *Scouting for Boys*, which **taught outdoor skills, self-discipline, and social responsibility**. The movement became known as the *Boy Scouts*, and, shortly afterward, in 1909, the *Girl Guide* movement was founded.

In 1912, *Juliette Gordon Low* established the *Girl Guides* in America, which became known as the *Girl Scouts*. She was a deaf woman who had been involved in <u>social causes</u> since her youth and **dedicated her life** to girls' education and leadership. Juliette created the worldwide *Thinking Day For Girl Scouts and Girl Guides* to celebrate international friendship and **foster global citizenship** among young women leaders.

Scouts have long been known for their **resistance efforts and peace initiatives.** *The Boy Scouts of America* (BSA) began integrating boys of color in the 1920s, a significant step toward equality. In 1956, *Dr. Martin Luther King Jr.* praised the Girl Scouts for promoting desegregation. And later, in 2013, Girl Scouts *Madison Vorva* and *Rhiannon Tomtishen* protested *Kelloggs'* use of palm oil, highlighting deforestation issues.

A push for **gender equality** in the Scouting movement came from *Sydney Ireland,* a preteen girl from New York whose brother was a Boy Scout. Sydney began campaigning to join the Boy Scouts at 11, and her efforts helped lead to the BSA admitting girls and renaming it *Scouts BSA* in 2018.

> Scouts have long been known for their resistance efforts and peace initiatives.

Scouting is now the **largest youth movement in the world,** with over 174 Scout organizations. Scouting continues to adapt and evolve today, with initiatives like *Messengers of Peace* that encourage Scouts to make the world and the community around them **a more peaceful and connected place.**

STUYVESANT HIGH SCHOOL STUDENT STRIKE

In early May 1913, a horde of *Stuyvesant High School* students rushed into their lunchroom, scattering tables, chairs, and broken dishes and singing a rowdy chorus of *Irving Berlin*'s comedic tune "Snookey Ookums." Their school, known as "Stuy," forbade students to take their lunch breaks outside its walls, but the boys were **fed up with the tight conditions in their packed and poorly ventilated basement lunchroom**, with its low ceiling and web of steamy pipes. Thousands of students, also frustrated by the <u>poor value</u> of the cafeteria's food, called for their right to independence and shouted,

"We want good lunch! We want fresh air!"

Their protest against the lunch policy had begun earlier that week, when many upper-level students had started their day at Stuy, Manhattan's **first manual-trade school for boys**, by refusing to sing the school's traditional **"staid old"** hymns during the opening assembly.

The New York Times reported that one unnamed boy explained their action by saying:

"We aren't young chickens just out of the eggshell. We don't walk around with our eyes shut."

They were striking for more **flexibility and freedom** outside the classroom, and the boy described how their long back-to-back classes with only a 23-minute lunch in a confined space made it difficult to return to their ironwork in the school's foundry. **"We're big enough to take care of ourselves,"** he said,

"and most of us are here for work."

After several days of students pushing through guards at the school's doors, **refusing to move off school steps,** and flipping furniture and mounting tables while singing popular tunes at lunch, Stuy's *Principal Von Nardoff* finally met with student representatives to discuss their demands. Although Von Nardoff invited students from the school's *Arista League,* an honor society within the school, to hear their complaints, he wrote of the concerns of over a thousand students as **"the opinions of a few dissatisfied** [and] **restless** [boys who] **fancied grievances."**

Although **the students returned** to singing traditional hymns in assembly and eating lunch in the basement, **their unity and lively protest remain legendary** in New York's history.

KOREA: TEENS LEAD THE FIGHT FOR INDEPENDENCE

"Mansei! ... Long live Korean independence!" exclaimed 16-year-old *Gwan-sun Yu* as she rushed into the streets of Japanese-occupied Seoul on March 1, 1919. A student at *Ewha Haktang*, a school founded to educate women in Korea in the late 1800s, Gwan-sun joined **thousands of Koreans protesting Japan's colonial rule**. Inspired by the rising wave of protests, she and her classmates decided to get involved in the movement for Korean self-rule.

MANSEI!

On March 5, Gwan-sun and four classmates marched to the Namdaemun, the city's oldest wooden gate, for another demonstration. There, they were **detained by police** until school authorities arranged for their release.

By March 10, the Japanese government had **closed Korean schools** to weaken the *March 1st Independence Movement*. With Ewha's doors shut, Gwan-sun left for her village, Yongdu-ri, where she deepened her activism by **canvassing with her family** to gain supporters. She encouraged people in nearby towns to join a rally on April 1 at Aunae

Marketplace. On that day, **3,000 people gathered** to demand sovereignty. Tragically, Japanese police fired on the crowd, killing 19 of the protestors, including Gwan-sun's mother and father. **Gwan-sun was arrested and imprisoned**.

The **police pressured Gwan-sun to confess** and betray her fellow organizers in exchange for a lighter penalty. When she refused, **she was tortured** and moved to another prison. Despite her pleas for a fair trial, she was sentenced to five years in jail without one.

But Gwan-sun didn't give up. She led a sizable prison protest on the first anniversary of the March 1st Movement. As punishment, officials threw her into an isolated underground cell. She wrote, **"Japan will fall ... My only regret is not being able to do more for my country."** Gwan-sun died in 1920 from injuries inflicted by beatings.

Korea won its independence in 1945, thanks to the **bravery of thousands of activists**, including Gwan-sun Yu, who is remembered as **"Korea's Joan of Arc"** for her courage and sacrifice.

CHILDREN'S CRUSADE FOR AMNESTY

Some time after World War I ended, there was a group of American children who still hadn't welcomed their fathers home. These men had not been killed in the conflict, but were political prisoners who had **chosen not to serve in the military** after being drafted or had **participated in anti-war unions or political groups**. They were jailed under the *Espionage Act of 1917*, which barred speech or activities seen as disloyal to the United States. The children and their moms started a movement to make people aware of how unfairly their loved ones were being treated.

On April 29, 1922, the *Children's Crusade* march became the movement's most well-known action, when the sons and daughters of the prisoners rallied together to call for *President Harding* to pardon and set them free. *Kate Richards O'Hare*, a socialist activist, stood in solidarity with the families of the imprisoned men and led the march. Kate had herself been **charged and jailed** under the Espionage Act for delivering protest speeches and was determined to fight for the freedom of these **men of conscience**. Kate likened the jailing of these prisoners to the women who were accused of being witches and persecuted during the Salem Witch trials of the 1600s.

Kate's own journey from imprisonment to receiving a pardon gave her fellow marchers hope as they gathered at the *White House* in Washington, DC, with large signs saying, **"Four Years Since I Saw My Daddy"** and **"Is Opinion a Crime in the U.S.A.?"**

To begin with, President Harding **refused to meet** with the young marchers and rebuffed their appeals because he didn't want to **appear to be influenced** by the public pressure and press coverage.

It took a long spring and summer of activism, but by August 1922, **14 fathers were released** from federal prison.

THE GENEVA DECLARATION OF THE RIGHTS OF THE CHILD

> "The only international language in the world is a child's cry,"

said the English humanitarian *Eglantyne Jebb*, about the **suffering of children in war zones**. Eglantyne had seen this suffering firsthand. In 1913, she traveled to Macedonia as a member of the *Macedonian Relief Fund* **to help starving farm workers and their families** affected by the *Second Balkan War*.

After World War I ended in 1918, Eglantyne and her sister *Dorothy* started the *Fight the Famine Council* to end the *Allied Naval Blockade* on Germany and Austria-Hungary, despite there being a ceasefire. The Allied blockade caused the deaths of many children. Even though she was **bombarded with moldy fruit** back home in England and branded a turncoat for helping children from **"enemy"** nations,

She was ... branded a turncoat for helping children from "enemy" nations.

Eglantyne kept on. She made **newspaper headlines** after passing out flyers and chalking messages onto the streets, resulting in her being arrested and fined. Remarkably, her **£5 fine was paid** by her judge, *Sir Archibald Bodkin*, as a show of support and encouragement.

Eglantyne ... made newspaper headlines after passing out flyers and chalking messages on to the streets, resulting in her being arrested and fined.

Roused by this experience, Eglantyne put the **research and planning skills** she learned in college into developing the Fight the Famine Council, earning the nickname *"White Flame"* from her friends for her **burning devotion to the cause**. The success of their campaign motivated the sisters to create the *Save the Children International Union* in 1920.

"WHITE FLAME"

In 1921, Eglantyne chartered the SS *Torcello*, a cargo steamer full of **600 tons of lifesaving food and medical supplies** to help children affected by unrest and hunger in Russia. Then, in 1923, she made history when she wrote a powerful document defending the importance of children's rights called **The Geneva Declaration of the Rights of the Child**.

A year later, it received approval from the *League of Nations*, an international organization founded after World War I to promote peace and cooperation among countries. Eglantyne's proclamation marked the first time that the basic rights of children to food, protection from abuse, and access to education were **recognized in international law**.

And her legacy didn't end there—not only would the United Nations use the Declaration as the foundation of their 1989 *Convention on the Rights of the Child*, but *Save the Children* has also grown into **one of the largest global children's charities**, continuing to advocate for the well-being and rights of children today.

THE EDELWEISS PIRATES

> "Our song is freedom, love, and life. We're the Pirates of the Edelweiss."

So went the forbidden tune sung by the teenage activists of the *Edelweiss Pirates* while they **resisted the tyranny of the Nazi Party** in 1930s Germany.

The Nazis aimed to uphold their regime by **molding young people to follow their beliefs.** They took over all German youth movements between 1933 and 1936 to prepare girls to serve strictly as wives and mothers and boys to be soldiers. Teens were expected to adopt rigid rules and bigoted racial ideals and **pledge obedience without question**. If they refused, they risked being shunned, imprisoned, or worse.

By 1936, **all non-disabled young people** between 13 (14 for girls) and 17 were required to join the military-style *Hitler Youth* or its counterpart, the *League of German Girls*. According to the leader of the Nazi Party, *Adolf Hitler*,

"Whoever has the youth has the future."

Yet rebel youth groups emerged to **liberate themselves and future generations** from Nazi control.

As the Nazis tightened their grip on power in the late 1930s, these networks of rebellious teens named themselves "Edelweiss Pirates" and **waged their own war** on the Hitler Youth. The Pirates were mostly working-class young people who wore Edelweiss flower pins as a sign of resistance. They often grew their hair long and dressed in American-inspired clothes. Turned off by the stiff Nazi drills and strict uniformity, they met in cafes and parks, hiked, rode bikes, and camped in the forest **to speak and move freely and trade information**.

The Pirates were **treated as "lazy" outcasts** for rejecting Nazi beliefs, but these young rebels were far from lazy. Beyond their **joyful defiance of the rules**, the Pirates fought Hitler Youth patrols, sabotaged weapons, shared anti-Nazi leaflets, derailed trains carrying weapons, and offered food and shelter to people escaping concentration camps.

Decades later, the Edelweiss Pirates were recognized as

"RIGHTEOUS AMONG THE NATIONS"

by Jerusalem's *Yad Vashem Holocaust memorial*—an honor given to non-Jewish people **who risked their lives to save Jews during the Holocaust**. This special recognition shows how brave and impactful their actions were in standing up to the Nazis.

THE AMERICAN YOUTH CONGRESS CLAIMS YOUTH POWER

"We have a right to life! We have a right to liberty!" proclaimed the students of the *American Youth Congress* (AYC) in their *"Declaration of the Rights of American Youth"* on July 4, 1936. On this Independence Day, they issued a bold call to action **demanding rights and opportunities for young people**.

The movement for youth rights began when the *National Student League* (NSL) was founded at the City College of New York in 1931. The NSL fought against censorship, opposed unfair expulsions of students, and protested against war. These efforts paved the way for the formation of the AYC in 1935. At a time when child labor was widespread and the economy was struggling, the AYC became the first multiracial, nationwide organization demanding **"full educational opportunities ... security in times of need, civil rights, religious freedom, and peace."**

Before the AYC, working-class youth, students, youth of color, the unemployed, and other underrepresented young people were **largely overlooked by the political system**. At that time, the voting age was 21. The AYC grew to include

over 4 million youth from 513 different student, religious, labor, peace, and political groups. They used a poster showing a **Black man and a white woman student** marching next to a white man holding a flag with the words

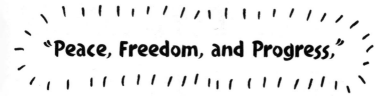

"Peace, Freedom, and Progress,"

to symbolize their commitment to unity.

The AYC demonstrated bold and effective organizing and showcased the power of young voices. Members of the AYC marched in Washington, DC, calling for more job opportunities and fair access to education. They resisted attacks from the *House Committee on Un-American Activities* and helped establish the *National Youth Administration*, a government program designed to provide job and education opportunities for young people. They also introduced the *American Youth Act* to the US Congress, which aimed to secure rights and opportunities for youth. Media attention and influential supporters, including *First Lady Eleanor Roosevelt*, helped garner support for their cause.

The AYC remained active until their leadership endorsed the *Molotov-Ribbentrop Pact*, a nonaggression treaty between the Soviet Union and Nazi Germany in 1939, just before World War II began. Their **support of the agreement caused a split** among their members and allies, leading to the organization's decline. Despite this, the AYC left a lasting legacy by highlighting the **importance of youth activism and the power of organized young voices**.

SWING YOUTH

In dancehalls across 1930s Europe, free-minded young people were **rejecting the culture of sameness** being forced upon them by the Nazi Party. Wearing wide-legged zoot suits and Hollywood make-up, *"Swing Boys"* and *"Swing Girls"* from an underground movement called the *"Swing Youth"* were embracing the lively swing style of American jazz music and dancing the Jitterbug **in rebellion**. In the eyes of the authorities, jazz and its African American roots were immoral.

Coming from working-class, middle-class, and wealthy backgrounds, Swings modeled themselves on "cool" musicians from the US. *Hans–Jürgen Massaquoi,* a Swing Boy with a German mother and Liberian father, said,

> "The Nazis hated our guts. Any chance they had, they would kick us in the pants."

Unlike the *Edelweiss Pirates*, who also rebelled against the culture of sameness but participated in political actions, the Swing Kids were **nonpolitical and culturally motivated**.

Young adults in this subculture called themselves Swing Youth as a snide reference to *Hitler Youth*, the hawkish youth organization run by the Nazi Party. The Jewish jazz guitarist *Coco Schumann*, a <u>Holocaust survivor</u> from Theresienstadt, noted that military marches and jazz share a rhythmic time. Still, people cannot march with military precision to jazz because it has an offbeat rhythm perfect for dancing—a nightmare for a state that **punished people for not conforming to their rules** by looking, being, and sounding uniform and rigid.

The Nazis banned jazz performances and radio programming and outlawed the sale of records from <u>Jewish and Black artists.</u> The *Gestapo*, the Nazis' secret state police, stormed into dancehalls in Hamburg and Berlin and **arrested masses of Swing Kids** out of disdain for their flashy outfits, carefree movement, Anglicisms, and cheeky mockery of Nazi rules. Many Swings were **detained and then sent home**, while others had their jazz records taken away and their hair cut as punishment. Some were even sent to **fight on the front lines of war or deported to forced labor camps**, which were often tantamount to concentration camps.

But although the Nazis attempted to **silence the Swing Youth**, the music played on, and locked-up Swing Boys and Girls often sang and **resisted together until liberation**.

THE WHITE ROSE

"Such a fine sunny day, and I have to go. But what does my death matter, if through us thousands of people are awakened and stirred to action?"

These were the last words of 21-year-old German *Sophie Scholl* before the Nazis executed her for **"treason"** on February 22, 1943. Sophie was killed because she belonged to the *White Rose*, **an anti-Nazi group despised by Hitler's Third Reich.**

Sophie's brother Hans, a medical student and former member of the *Hitler Youth*, founded the **nonviolent resistance group** the White Rose in 1942 with other students, including *Christoph Probst, Willi Graf*, and *Alexander Schmorell*. Hans had **started to doubt the regime** after taking university classes on Christian ethics that challenged Nazi ideals and observing the abuse of Jewish forced laborers while serving in the German army.

The involvement of everyday Germans in the Nazi's grisly crimes troubled the White Rose. Outraged that **people knew Jews were murdered and failed to act**, the group hoped an appeal to their humanity through leaflets and graffiti might inspire rebellion. They diligently copied leaflets with a stencil duplicator and distributed them in 1942. And, after the **defeat of the German armed forces** at the *Battle of Stalingrad* in Russia in 1943, they called for other students to resist: **"We will not be silent. We are your bad conscience. The White Rose will not leave you in peace!"** The White Rose expanded into other cities until their leaders were arrested and faced corrupt trials in 1943. Alongside Sophie, Hans and Christoph were also executed.

A hero of freedom and humanity.

In 2019, *Traute Lafrenz*, the **last surviving member** of the White Rose, was awarded Germany's highest civilian honor as a **"hero of freedom and humanity."** Lafrenz had escaped likely death when her prison was **liberated by the Allies** only three days before her trial was set to begin.

The White Rose demonstrated that everyone is in a position to contribute to the overthrow of an unjust system. **Their legacy of dissent in the face of injustice endures.**

"We will not be silent. We are your bad conscience. The White Rose will not leave you in peace!"

THE GREEN FEATHER MOVEMENT

In 1954, Indiana University students Edwin Napier, Bernard Bray, Mary Dawson, Blas Davila, and Jeanine Carter started the *Green Feather Movement* to **protest a book-banning campaign** targeting Robin Hood. *Mrs Thomas J. White*, a reviewer for the Indiana Textbook Commission, claimed the legend of Robin Hood encouraged communist thinking and threatened social order.

This was the era of McCarthyism, a time when the government, led by the actions of *Senator Joseph McCarthy*, was intensely fearful of communism. The FBI, under *J. Edgar Hoover*, spied on people suspected of having communist sympathies using wiretaps and informers. Public **fear of communism was high**, and between 1950 and 1954, college students **protested against** these unfair accusations.

Motivated by their **belief in free speech** and inspired by discussions at their Baptist church, the Indiana students took action. As their symbol they used green feathers, like those worn by *Robin Hood*. Despite the risk of blowback, they spread huge burlap bags full of **dyed green chicken feathers** across their campus.

Backlash did follow. Critics **condemned and scrutinized** the students, particularly when youth from campuses in multiple states began wearing green feather pins to show their support.

The *Green Feather Movement* lasted two semesters and spread to universities on both coasts and the American Midwest. Stories about the students' efforts reached *Sherwood Forest* in England, Robin Hood's legendary hideout. *The New York Times* covered the local response to Mrs White with the headline **"Sherwood Forest Laughs."** Ultimately, White's campaign to ban *Robin Hood* failed.

LITTLE ROCK NINE

September 1957 was the start of high school for *Melba Pattillo, Ernest Green, Elizabeth Eckford, Minnijean Brown, Terrence Roberts, Carlotta Walls, Jefferson Thomas, Gloria Ray,* and *Thelma Mothershed*. But when these **nine African American students tried to enter** the <u>formerly all-white</u> Central High in Little Rock, the Arkansas National Guard **blocked them**.

In addition to troops, the students were met by a vicious mob who threw objects and shouted taunts.

> "Two, four, six, eight! We don't want to integrate!"

yelled the crowd. White teen *Hazel Bryan* was captured in an infamous photo, screaming at Elizabeth Eckford. Newspapers reported that Bryan said, **"Go home! Go back to Africa!"** along with a slur.

The Supreme Court ruled that the **segregation** of public schools was <u>unconstitutional</u> in 1954. However, *Governor Orval Faubus* still ordered the state's National Guard to prevent the nine students from accessing their new school. Faubus claimed that he did it to **"maintain order,"** but instead, he was determined to hold back integration and disrupt progress. Faubus wanted to be seen as a champion of segregation by voters.

Faubus ignored *President Eisenhower*'s requests to let the *Little Rock Nine* into school, so the president sent federal troops and **took the local National Guard under federal control.**

At Central High, the Nine **endured hostility**, including hitting, name-calling, death threats, and acid attacks. Some of the students found thumbtacks on their chairs, had to duck when fiery balls of paper were tossed over bathroom stalls, and survived gunshots being blasted through the windows of their homes.

Ernest Green became Central's first Black graduate in May 1958, and *Dr. Martin Luther King Jr.* watched him receive his diploma. In September of that year, Faubus **closed all Little Rock's schools to halt further integration**. In a vote, 19,470 to 7,561 decided to keep schools closed. Central High's doors remained shut to an integrated student population **until 1960.**

The Little Rock Nine were recognized with the Congressional Gold Medal in 1999. Their heroism earned global attention and paved the way for movements that continue **to fight for educational equality and anti-racism** today.

REBELS WITH A CAUSE: YOUNG LEADERS CHANGE THE COURSE OF HISTORY

In April 1960, students from over 50 colleges and high schools gathered at *Shaw University*, a historically Black college in North Carolina, for the *Southern Youth Leadership Conference*. This call to action came from

Ella Baker, an alumna of Shaw, and *Dr. Martin Luther King Jr.*, both of whom fiercely believed in the **power of students to lead the movement for freedom** from the brutally oppressive and cruel *Jim Crow laws* of the time.

Jim Crow laws existed for about a century, from the *post–Civil War* era until 1968. These laws were **designed to exclude and belittle African Americans** by denying them the right to vote, blocking them from using public transportation fairly, and limiting their access to jobs and education. These laws forced Black people to drink from separate water fountains and use **"colored-only"** bathrooms, beaches, and pools.

At Shaw, organizers discussed their strategies, shared ideas about future campaigns, and created the *Student Nonviolent Coordinating Committee* (SNCC, pronounced **"snick"**). One of the students attending, *Diane Nash*, said,

> "We felt a real kinship with the students who were working in other cities to bring about the same things that we were."

The conference's biggest bloc of students came from Nashville, Tennessee, including 20-year-old *John Lewis*, whose motto was **"Get in Good Trouble."** The Nashville delegation had been mentored by *James Morris Lawson Jr.*, a key architect of the Civil Rights Movement who studied

Mahatma Gandhi's philosophy in India. Gandhi believed **nonviolent resistance is always more moral, effective, and just than physical force or cruelty.**

Following the urging of the Nashville students, SNCC **embraced nonviolence** as a core principle.

John Lewis helped build the SNCC and **risked his life** to engage in peaceful actions, including serving as one of 13 initial Black and white *Freedom Riders* in May 1961. The *Freedom Rides* were bus trips taken by Black and white activists throughout the South to **protest segregation** in **"whites-only"** bus terminal bathrooms, restaurants, and waiting areas.

John's bus set off for New Orleans, Louisiana, from Washington, DC, but the riders were **brutally attacked by vicious white mobs and arrested**. Lewis recalled that he thought he would die after being knocked out and left on the ground in an Alabama bus station. **But he kept going.**

John became chairman of the SNCC in 1963. That same year, he made history as the youngest speaker at the *March on Washington for Jobs and Freedom*. In front of a 250,000-person crowd, he pushed the president and Congress to enact the *Civil Rights Act* to **outlaw discrimination based on race, color, religion, sex, and national origin.**

Ella Baker ... and Dr. Martin Luther King Jr. ... fiercely believed in the power of students to lead the movement for freedom from the brutally oppressive and cruel Jim Crow laws of the time.

Under John's leadership, the SNCC played a major role in many significant actions, including organizing *Freedom Summer* in 1964 to **spotlight Mississippi's racism** and to help register Black voters. His leadership and dedication impacted the Civil Rights Movement and American society, **paving the way for future generations** to continue the fight for equality.

"GET IN GOOD TROUBLE"

SIT-IN REVOLUTION: STUDENTS TURN THE TABLES ON INJUSTICE

On February 1, 1960, four Black college students, *Ezell Blair Jr.* (now Jibreel Khazan), *Franklin McCain, Joseph McNeil,* and *David Richmond*, peacefully sat down at the 66-seat lunch counter in a Woolworths store in Greensboro, North Carolina. In the early 1960s, **segregation was still commonplace** throughout the American South, and Jim Crow policies meant many lunch counters, drugstores, and other public spaces **refused to serve Black and white patrons together**.

In the Greensboro Woolworths restaurant, Black customers were forced to stand at a snack bar to eat, while white customers were given the right to sit while dining. But the *Greensboro Four* chose to sit, even though **staff barred them from ordering and the manager called the police.** News of their action spread rapidly, and more than 300 protesters packed into the store four days later, causing the media and the American public to take notice.

The foursome was prepared for this response. After Franklin had been denied the right to buy a hotdog at a segregated counter the previous year, the four men had

made a plan to use nonviolent activism

to build public awareness and advance their cause. And they would be building on **a model of protest** going back to Virginia in 1939, when Black attorney *Samuel Wilbert Tucker* **organized a sit-in** at the Alexandria Library. Although the Greensboro Four knew they would be **faced with hostility**, they were determined to return to Woolworths for as many days as it took to make an impact.

Meanwhile, in Nashville, students launched their own **sit-in campaign** from February to May of 1960, with actions at bus terminals, department stores, and other locations. The Nashville students **faced brutal violence, arrest, and other hardships,** but their actions led to the Nashville merchant boycott, a massive march to City Hall, and eventually, the desegregation of lunch counters downtown.

It also brought Fisk University students *Diane Nash, C. T. Vivian, James Bevel,* and *John Lewis* into national view as changemakers and **promising young leaders** in nonviolent resistance. Before the sit-ins, the students had engaged in **nonviolence workshops** taught by Vanderbilt Divinity School student *James Lawson,* who also participated in the organization of the sit-ins. This action later led to his expulsion from Vanderbilt in 1960.

Back in Greensboro, thanks to the protestors, several Woolworths stores **opened their doors to all customers** and were **desegregated**, despite bullying, harassment, bombing, beatings, and arrests.

The Nashville students faced brutal violence, arrest, and other hardships.

The Greensboro and Nashville sit-ins were not just isolated events, but <u>critical moments</u> in the Civil Rights Movement. Their actions **inspired 70,000 people to participate in their own sit-ins between 1960 and 1964,** marking a significant shift in the fight against segregation.

BIRMINGHAM CHILDREN'S CRUSADE

RING! RING!

Fire bells rang out from schools across Birmingham, Alabama, as children pulled alarms and opened windows to signal that it was time to gather for their **mighty walkout and march against segregation**. The aim on May 2, 1963, was to get as many students as possible to protest the unjust laws that did not grant <u>equal rights</u> and access to services to Black Americans in Birmingham.

Just four months earlier, Alabama's governor *George Wallace* stood to speak at his January 14, 1963, inaugural speech in Montgomery, at the site where *Jefferson Davis* (the defeated Confederate States of America president) was sworn in. Wallace's voice boomed,

> "Segregation now, segregation tomorrow, segregation forever"

to thunderous applause from a **crowd of white supporters of his divisive policies**. Wallace <u>vowed to block laws</u> that would ban school segregation, sending sparks flying and **igniting hostility** that called advocates for justice and equality to action.

On May 2, more than a thousand courageous school-age children who were trained in the **protest method of nonviolent direct action** by the *Southern Christian Leadership Conference* skipped their classes on what they called **"D-Day."** They were headed to 16th Street Baptist Church to defy George Wallace's promise to allow segregation to continue by <u>marching together</u>.

The protesters gathered in groups of 10 to 50 outside the church with handwritten signs that said, **"Can a man love God and hate his brother?"** and sang songs, including these words: **"I woke up this morning with my mind set on freedom."** They chanted,

CAN A MAN LOVE GOD AND HATE HIS BROTHER?

"Wallace, you can never jail us. Segregation is bound to fail."

Arrests began as the children marched in two big groups. The police summoned more officers after taking **at least 600 children**—some as young as 7—in police vans and buses before jailing them.

Still, that didn't stop the brave children! On May 3, hundreds more students gathered at the church to march peacefully.

FREEDOM!

But staunch segregationist and leader of Birmingham's police and fire departments, *Eugene "Bull" Connor*, attacked the protesters with **ferocious police dogs** and slammed the children with intense water pressure from **fire hoses**. Only 10 children remained standing as their peers were toppled, but their song could not be silenced. **"Freedom!"** they cried out above the commotion as bystanders watched the terror.

Journalists captured the brutality for the nation to witness, leading to bad press and increased pressure on lawmakers in Birmingham and Alabama to end segregation. The children's courageous actions helped pave the way for support from *President John F. Kennedy* and, later, the passing of the Civil Rights Act of 1964, which finally **outlawed unjust discrimination and segregation** in the United States of America.

Decades later, in an Academy Award-winning film called *Mighty Times: The Children's March*, *Reverend Gwen Webb*, who had been one of the brave young Birmingham activists, said,

"People thought the kids were going to get hurt, but the reality was that we were born Black in Alabama, and we were going to get hurt if we didn't do something."

COURAGE IN THE CLASSROOM: NYC SCHOOL BOYCOTTS

After 1920, **school segregation was illegal** in New York City. However, due to unfair housing policies, children were still mostly kept apart based on race and ethnicity. *Freedom Day*, also known as the *New York School Boycott*, was held on February 3, 1964, **to protest this segregation** in New York City's public schools. Thousands of children joined the strike, shouting,

"Jim Crow must go!"

and "Integration means better schools for all!" Students at Harlem's PS 121 made homemade signs expressing their needs:

WE WANT A CLEAN BATHROOM AND SCHOOL

GIVE ME A BETTER SCHOOL PLEASE

GIVE US A CHANCE TO LEARN IN SMALLER GROUPS

Before the boycott, the *Board of Education* had introduced a three-year plan to rezone and reduce overcrowding in schools serving Black and Latino/Latine/Latinx children. However, **racial justice activists** argued the plan needed to be stronger.

Parents and Taxpayers, a mainly white organization, urged students to attend schools closest to their homes while opposing bussing with slogans like **"Bussing Creates Fussing."** Bussing involved transporting students to **schools within or outside their local districts to support integration**.

BUSSING CREATES FUSSING

Over **half a million people**, including around 460,000 students and teachers, participated in school boycotts to protest against school segregation, inadequate funding, and to demand fair and quality education for all. *Reverend Milton Galamison*, chair of the *Committee for Integrated Schools*, led the boycott with the help of *March on Washington* strategist *Bayard Rustin*. Organizations including the NAACP, Congress of Racial Equality, National Urban League, Harlem Parents' Committee, and Parents' Workshop for Equality supported the campaign.

The **activism and determination** of these students, parents, and organizations eventually led to major changes. Although there were setbacks, their efforts helped pave the way for more integrated and equitable education in New York City and beyond.

BERKELEY FREE SPEECH MOVEMENTS

On December 2, 1964, a crowd of **4,000 protestors**, mainly college students aged between 18 and 24, gathered in Sproul Plaza, Berkeley, California. They were **listening to the bold words** of *Mario Savio*, a 21-year-old Italian American philosophy student from Queens, New York.

Savio urged the crowd to use the power of civil disobedience to make a difference after a large protest at the *University of California, Berkeley* campus sparked the *Free Speech Movement*. This movement aimed to secure the right to **free speech and academic freedom** on campus, but it had resulted in a **university-wide ban on political activities**. He demanded that the university administration lift the ban and recognize students' rights, declaring,

> "You've got to make it stop! And you've got to indicate to the people who run it ... that unless you're free the machine will be prevented from working at all."

Mario Savio was passionate about organizing for civil rights causes. In the fall of 1963, he transferred from *Manhattan College* to the University of California, Berkeley. In addition to his studies, he devoted his time to **anti-racist activism**, particularly responding to the *San Francisco Hotel Association's* **refusal to hire African Americans** for jobs outside of maintenance and housekeeping.

Savio delivered his now-famous **"Bodies Upon the Gears"** speech from the steps of Berkeley's *Sproul Hall* with fierce passion. Describing a meeting he had with university officials, Savio compared the university president to a corporation chief. Then, as students marched inside to sit in, famous folk singer *Joan Baez* sang the gospel and civil-rights era protest song

"WE SHALL OVERCOME."

The Free Speech Movement inspired many student protests of the 1960s, 1970s, and onward. The Sproul Plaza steps, where Savio's words stirred thousands to action, continue to symbolize the **fight for free speech**. They were renamed the *"Mario Savio Steps"* in 1997 as **a tribute to his legacy**, and have been a site for highly visible anti-Vietnam War protests, women's rights rallies in the 1970s, South African anti-apartheid actions in the 1980s, *"Occupy Cal"* protests in 2011, climate strikes, and the *"Gaza Solidarity Encampment"* in 2024.

STUDENTS LIBERATE LEARNING AT FREEDOM SCHOOLS

Many African Americans and low-income whites in 1960s Mississippi **lacked fair access to voting** and the information and resources needed to organize and advocate for change. In 1963, while the *Student Nonviolent Coordinating Committee* (SNCC) was planning for *Freedom Summer*, activist *Charles Cobb* <u>wrote a memo</u> urging his organization to sponsor a Freedom Schools network. The goal was to use education to help African Americans **gain political, cultural, social, and economic equality and justice**.

Cobb called on his peers to use their organization to help the most excluded and marginalized Mississippians to

"articulate their own desires, demands, and questions"

and to **"find ... new directions for action."** True to Cobb's goal, Freedom Schools offered **a new alternative and progressive path** for Black Mississippians. Over 10 weeks, white students partnered with local Black civil rights activists in Mississippi **to register Black voters and fight discrimination** by teaching civics, history, reading, writing, and math classes. As the **media took note** of the stories emerging from these temporary but enduring schools, they also became aware of the brutal violence and injustice occurring in Mississippi. This **raised awareness and support** for the cause across the nation.

Joyce Brown, a 16-year-old Mississippian, attended a Freedom School in McComb. In 1964, the school was bombed. Joyce wrote a poem about her dedication to keeping the work of her school going. Although she was **angry about the act of racist terrorism** her community had experienced, she vowed to continue **advocating for justice**. In her poem, Joyce declared,

> "Here I have come, and here
> I shall stay, and no amount of fear
> my determination can sway ..."

Her community heeded the call, came together, and found a new site for what then **became one of the most powerful Freedom Schools** in the state.

As a result of their efforts, over 2,500 people of all ages—including teens, their parents, and grandparents—were **better prepared to vote, organize, become elected officials**, and encourage others to act.

STUDENT WALKOUTS SHAKE THE LA SCHOOL SYSTEM

"WALKOUT!"

was the rallying cry of about 15,000 Mexican American students who were fed up with **unjust treatment and terrible conditions** in their Los Angeles schools in March of 1968. High drop-out rates, staff shortages, overcrowded classrooms, textbooks that erased Chicano history, and some teachers using racist slurs **motivated students, educators, and their allies to stage walkouts.**

Youth carrying signs with slogans like "Is Education A Crime?" and "Unite for Better Schools" gathered in large numbers. Some students chanted "¡Viva La Revolución!" in Spanish to **show pride in their culture,** language, and background. On their way to walking out, they drummed on lockers while chanting and giving speeches about their **right to a better education.** When police arrived and tried to stop them with violence and bullying, the students stood their ground. They served as **guardians and protectors for each other,** with some youths acting as shields to protect their fellow students. *Luis Torres*, one of the young activists, described their movement as

> "Brainiacs, jocks, cheerleaders, nerds, and gangbangers, all marching together."

Authorities pressured students to stop exposing injustice in their schools. The students responded with demands, including that **no one should be punished** for joining the protest. Before the walkouts, the director of the *United States Federal Bureau of Investigation, J. Edgar Hoover*, had written a memo calling for a block on **"minority"** movements, so these Chicano students were worried about **what punishment might follow for them.**

Despite her father's concerns that the authorities' response to her activism might prevent her from graduating, *Paula Crisostomo*, a 17-year-old firstborn daughter of eight from the *Boyle Heights housing project*, pressed on as one of the **movement's core leaders**. Another organizer, *Harry Gamboa Jr.*, an artist and student government member, was labeled by the government as

"one of the hundred most dangerous and violent subversives in the United States."

Still, the students refused to give up, and 13 organizers known as the *East LA 13* were arrested. *Sal Castro*, a teacher and protest organizer, was fired. By 1970, the **charges against all the students were dropped**, and Castro's job was restored after the community organized sit-ins against his removal.

STUDENT VOICES ROAR WORLDWIDE

The year 1968 was a turning point for young people worldwide. Between January 1968 and March 1969, **youth-driven rebellions** against dictatorships, authoritarianism, inequality, injustice, the military draft, and civil and human rights violations <u>raged across the globe.</u> In some cases, the protests emerged to counter government policy actions. Others focused on labor conditions, gender justice, free expression, and defying traditional values that clashed with the next generation's vision for the future. **Nowhere was more rebellious than France.**

> # "BE REALISTIC; DEMAND THE IMPOSSIBLE."

In 1968, **students** revolted in the French capital, Paris.

"Be realistic; demand the impossible."
"It is forbidden to forbid. Let your imagination rule."

These slogans, made famous by the French 1968 student protest movement, called on people to realize their dreams for their communities instead of accepting the status quo. Students marched, went on strike, and occupied factories and universities throughout the country for <u>almost two months</u> in May 1968.

As students took to the streets, factory workers walked out and staged sit-ins **to demand change**. In one of the most intense periods of <u>European unrest</u> since World War II, France saw one of the biggest mass protests of the year. *President Charles de Gaulle* pushed to **crush the uprising**, leading to street fights between protestors and the police. France's trade unions staged strikes **in sympathy** with the protestors. As France's first nationwide wildcat general strike, it was the largest ever attempted, with **10 million people** involved.

France was driven to a standstill. Politicians feared civil war or revolution. President Charles de Gaulle secretly left France for West Germany, **imposing a momentary halt on the national government**. His whereabouts were unknown for hours. To ensure support if troops were needed to retake Paris, de Gaulle met with *General Jacques Massu*, commander of the French occupation forces, to discuss the revolt's impact.

> ## Politicians feared civil war or revolution.

1968 was also pivotal for the *Civil Rights Movement* in the United States. Membership of *The Black Panther Party*, founded by students *Huey P. Newton* and *Bobby Seale*, grew to around 2,000. The movement saw an upsurge of university **students focusing on political action**, including strikes.

And, **in that same rebellious year**, youth organized civil rights and free speech rallies and strikes in countries including Poland, Mexico, and the former Yugoslavia. **Protests against** the *Vietnam War* increased in the United States, Berlin, London, Rome, and other cities. And **tensions heightened** between Northern Ireland's Protestant majority and the

Catholic minority, leading to the sectarian conflict known as *The Troubles*.

In that same rebellious year, youth organized civil rights and free speech rallies and strikes in countries including Poland, Mexico, and the former Yugoslavia.

In addition to impacting policy and public discussion, the **youth-driven actions of 1968 influenced** protest art and storytelling, shaping street art, songs, posters, and emergent movements **for more than half a century**.

PEOPLE'S DEMOCRACY

"We were born into an unjust system; we are not prepared to grow old in it," said *Bernadette Devlin*, a Belfast student and member of *People's Democracy*, a student-led grassroots political organization from the Northern Irish civil rights movement that began in 1968.

This period, known as *The Troubles*, saw **30 years of conflict over whether Northern Ireland should stay in the United Kingdom or join the Republic of Ireland**. The divide was often along religious lines: most *Irish Catholics* wanted a united Ireland free from British colonial rule, while most *Protestants* preferred to remain part of the UK.

People's Democracy **stood up against British rule** for fair jobs and housing, freedom of speech and protest, and voting rights. In 1969, Bernadette was **elected to the British Parliament**, becoming the youngest MP ever, at that point. Jailed for her role in the *Battle of the Bogside* in 1970, Bernadette became widely known for her involvement in the clash that highlighted the struggle for justice in Northern Ireland.

Bernadette's activism also drew international attention. During a 1969 tour of the United States, she connected with the *Black Panther Party*, recognizing **shared struggles** for civil

"We were born into an unjust system; we are not prepared to grow old in it."

rights. During her tour, she gave the Black Panthers a golden key to New York City, which she had received as a result of her work, as **a show of support and solidarity**.

Tensions peaked in 1972 on *"Bloody Sunday,"* when British soldiers **killed 13 unarmed protestors** in Derry, Northern Ireland. Bernadette, present at the march, confronted the *Home Secretary* in Parliament for **misrepresenting the incident** as the fault of the protestors.

The Troubles resulted in **around 3,600 deaths**, affecting civilians, British soldiers, and guerrilla fighters like the *Irish Republican Army* (IRA), who also sought a united Ireland. A peace deal, the **Good Friday Agreement**, was reached on April 10, 1998.

BRIGHTER FUTURE

Voters in Northern Ireland **supported the end of direct rule by the UK**, leading to the creation of the *Northern Ireland Assembly*, which could make decisions on some issues without getting permission from Parliament. The Republic of Ireland **amended its constitution to remove its territorial claim over Northern Ireland**, fostering a more peaceful relationship and contributing to the end of the conflict.

Many young people in Northern Ireland saw it as a step toward a brighter future.

TINKER V. DES MOINES

END THE **WAR NOW!** BRING THE TROOPS HOME

Mary Beth Tinker, a 13-year-old Des Moines, Iowa, student went to school on December 16, 1965, wearing a **black armband with a white peace sign**. Over two dozen elementary, middle, and high school students from Des

Moines, including *Bruce Clark*, *Christopher Eckhardt*, and Mary Beth's siblings *John*, *Hope*, and *Paul*, joined her in **wearing armbands to protest the Vietnam War.**

Mary Beth was **inspired to act** after her parents traveled to Mississippi to register Black voters during the *Freedom Summer* movement of the previous year. Their stories about volunteering on the front lines of the Civil Rights Movement motivated the 13-year-old to make her mark on history.

"By Christmas of 1965, it was my turn to speak up,"

Mary Beth said of the Vietnam War.

"Watching burning huts and soldiers in body bags on TV, my brothers and sisters and I joined other students to wear black armbands to mourn the dead."

The students were sent home after **they refused to remove the bands** and were suspended. They received menacing calls and threats, and one day, red paint was daubed on the Tinker home.

The *American Civil Liberties Union* (ACLU) supported Mary Beth, her classmates, and their families in their four-year legal fight against the *Des Moines Independent Community School District* for the **right to protest**. In the 1969 *Tinker v. Des Moines* court case, the *Supreme Court* ruled 7-2 in favor of the students, saying they did not

"shed their constitutional rights to freedom of speech or expression at the schoolhouse gate."

The court decided that students were <u>entitled to free speech</u> unless it disrupted education, and armbands were deemed **nondisruptive**. Their case had been helped by *Burnside* v. *Byars* from 1966, in which **the court ruled in favor of students' First Amendment rights on school grounds** after students at an all-Black high school in Philadelphia, Mississippi, were disciplined for wearing anti-racist and voter rights buttons. **Both milestone rulings are still cited in cases today**.

In 2006, the ACLU named the *Mary Beth Tinker Youth Involvement Award* after the youth rights activist and retired nurse practitioner.

BREAKING GENDER BARRIERS AT STUYVESANT HIGH

Alice de Rivera, a 13-year-old at the top of her class, scored a remarkable **99 out of 100** on New York City's mathematics test. Aiming for a school that matched her high-level abilities, Alice wanted to apply to *Stuyvesant High School*, a specialized school known for its rigorous academic programs. However, she was **denied the chance to take the entrance exam because she was a girl**.

In 1969, Alice, a *John Jay High School* freshman, sued the *Board of Education* for gender discrimination. A media outlet covering her case nicknamed her

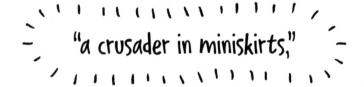

"a crusader in miniskirts,"

focusing more on her appearance than her **intellect and skills**. In May 1969, rather than go to court, the Board of Education **repealed the gender restriction** at Stuyvesant. Alice did not attend Stuyvesant because her family moved upstate after the trial, but 12 girls started at the school in the fall of 1969.

At first, there were **no facilities for girls**. In one bathroom, urinals were covered with boards, and a temporary "Girls" sign was placed over the **"Boys"** sign on the door. Some staff members, accustomed to teaching only boys, were **uncomfortable interacting with the new female students. Despite these challenges**, 223 girls enrolled in 1970.

Alice, the great-great-granddaughter of suffragist *Eugenie de Rivera*, made her **own mark as a trailblazer**, opening doors for others to have more equal opportunities. Thanks to her efforts, other schools in the area were **forced to address bias in their application processes**. Over 40 years later, in 2013, Stuyvesant High School awarded Alice an honorary diploma.

> She was denied the chance to take the entrance exam because she was a girl.

Today, **girls make up more than 40%** of the student body, but questions about equity and race in the admission process are still being debated.

HIGH SCHOOL WOMEN'S COALITION

Hariette Surovell, a 16-year-old high school student from New York City, spoke on behalf of the *High School Women's Coalition* before *President Nixon's* **National Commission on Population Growth and the American Future** in 1971. She addressed the presidential advisory group formed after Nixon delivered his 1969 "Message on Population," predicting that the United States population could grow to **300 million** by 2000. He said,

"This growth will produce serious challenges for our society ... many of our present social problems may be related to the fact that we have had only 50 years ... to accommodate the second hundred million Americans."

Hariette spoke about how young women from across New York City were organizing meetings and **"rap rooms"** (a slang term used at the time for informal discussion groups) to talk about their daily realities as students without ample **access to relevant reproductive health courses**. She expressed her frustration to the commission that her school's **lack of family planning information** likely resulted in a classmate becoming pregnant.

Since her school **refused to provide education** about birth control, Hariette had passed out handbooks diagramming the reproductive system and leaflets about pregnancy testing until **a teacher blocked her campaign**. She told the commission that when word got around the school, the leaflets **"went like hotcakes."** She said,

> **"I would bring stacks of literature, and by the end of the school day, it had disappeared."**

Hariette and the High School Women's Coalition went on to rally the *Board of Education* to create a program to educate youth about **birth control and sexually transmitted disease prevention**. Three thousand people signed a petition in support of the coalition, which blamed the problem of teen pregnancies on scarce scientific education and outdated lesson plans.

"How can high school girls be expected to be responsible about using birth control when all knowledge is gotten on the street? Many don't even have a clear picture of how babies are made,"

Hariette said.

The coalition's efforts paid off. Later in 1971, the commission called for improved conditions, services, and education through schools, community groups, and mentoring programs for **"teens teaching teens"**—just as Hariette had done for her classmates.

SOUTH AFRICAN YOUTH ACTIVIST MOVEMENTS

As the morning sun rose over the township of Soweto in South Africa on June 16, 1976, tension and anticipation filled the air. **Students gathered, armed only with their voices** and an unwavering determination, **in defiance of the authorities**. Led by *Teboho "Tsietsi" Mashinini*, they marched purposefully, their chants echoing like a thunderous drumbeat of dissent.

This was the Soweto Youth Uprising, now considered one of the most important events in South Africa's history. Thousands of young South Africans took to the streets to protest the government's decision to **enforce Afrikaans as the language** used in schools. To these spirited youth, it wasn't just about language; it was about their identity, heritage, and the right to an education, justice, and equality that honored their cultures.

> Students gathered, armed only with their voices and an unwavering determination, in defiance of the authorities.

However, the **peaceful demonstration was met with brute force** as the police opened fire on the unarmed protesters, leaving a trail of devastation in their wake. Among the casualties of the police gunfire was *Hector Pieterson*, a schoolboy whose **tragic death symbolized the brutality of apartheid**. Hector's haunting photograph, broadcast worldwide, served as a **stark reminder of the horrors** the people of Soweto faced in their struggle for justice and freedom.

Apartheid, **a system of racial segregation and discrimination**, deeply affected the lives of South Africans every day. Townships like Soweto were areas designated for

Black residents, **separated from white communities by law** and enforced with brutal punishments. This segregation was a key element of apartheid, making life extremely difficult for Black, Colored, Indian, and other South Africans who were **not afforded equal rights with white people** in South Africa between 1948 and 1994.

Decades later, the **courage and defiance** of those young activists resonate in the work of South Africa's youth today. *Zulaikha Patel*, born after apartheid ended, became famous at a young age for challenging **discriminatory policies** at *Pretoria Girls High School* that targeted Black students' natural hair.

While Zulaikha's protest sparked a **national conversation** about race, identity, and equality in education, another movement called *Rhodes Must Fall* gained momentum at the *University of Cape Town*. Led by passionate activists like *Sizwe Mpofu-Walsh*, the goal was to remove symbols that glorified colonial figures such as *Cecil Rhodes*, a British imperialist and politician. An imperialist is someone who believes in extending their country's power and influence over other countries, often by taking control of them and exploiting their resources. The movement was not just about tearing down statues that represented the violent and racist history of apartheid, but also about **confronting the lingering legacies of colonialism and injustice** that continue to impact South African society.

The movement was not just about tearing down statues ... but also about confronting the lingering legacies of colonialism and injustice that continue to impact South African society.

Today in South Africa, *Youth Day* is celebrated every June 16 in honor of the thousands of students who took to the streets of Soweto to protest in 1976. As the torchbearers of a new generation, **youth activists carry forward the legacy** of those who came before them, inspiring future generations to **continue the fight for a more just society**.

NEPALESE YOUTH MARCH FOR CHANGE

In April 1979, Nepal was under Panchayat rule, a strict system in which **political parties were banned** and people had to follow the motto "One King, One Dress, One Language, One Nation." The **revolution began when students protested** against military dictator *Zia-ul-Haq*'s hanging of Pakistani *Prime Minister Zulfikar Ali Bhutto.*

ONE KING,
ONE DRESS,
ONE LANGUAGE,
ONE NATION

As the protesters marched toward the Pakistani embassy in Kathmandu, **riot police confronted them**. The situation turned violent, with protesters burning a government newspaper office and a gas station while police used batons and tear gas. **Eleven people died, and over 150 were injured.**

"To change the face of the nation, rise up!"

The students were not just angry about Bhutto's death; they also **demanded their rights**, including press freedom and free speech. Some students boycotted classes, and others clashed with authorities. *Shyam Tamot*, a student from

Mahendra College, wrote a song called **"Rise, Rise from the Village,"** which became the anthem of the protestors, inspiring them to sing, **"To change the face of the nation, rise up!"** in the streets of Kathmandu Valley.

Student leaders created a **list of over 20 demands**, seeking an end to repression and *a more representative government*. Although authorities shut down campuses to stop the protests, the uprisings spread to 40 districts.

By May, the **education minister had been replaced**, and campuses had reopened. The Nepalese royals and student committees **reached an agreement**, freeing 160 arrested students and 64 political prisoners. They also decided to end university entrance exams, increase merit scholarships, and allow independent unions.

Most importantly, *King Birendra* announced a referendum on whether political parties should be allowed in Nepal. The *Nepalese Democracy Movement* will forever be remembered for the **role students played in making a lasting impact**. Today, Nepal has many political parties and a parliament, and since 2015, it has been called the *Federal Democratic Republic of Nepal*.

IRANIAN REVOLUTION

In 1979, Iran was swept up in a wave of fervor and rebellion. Fed up with *Mohammad Reza Shah Pahlavi*'s rule, crowds largely made up of **young activists took to the streets** in protest, with universities at the center of the change.

The youth were frustrated. As they demanded change, their **collective voice of protest** grew louder, and the Shah was <u>forced to flee</u> the country. The rise of the next leader of Iran, *Ayatollah Khomeini,* and the establishment of the Islamic Republic of Iran were **turning points that shaped the next generation of Iranians**.

The rebellion's roots can be traced back to the 1953 US-backed coup, a pivotal event that handed power to Mohammad Reza Shah Pahlavi and **sparked increased activism** among Iran's youth and Islamic groups. The Shah's reliance on US arms and aid further rocked the foundation of Iranian society, fueling the spread of dissent and **setting the stage for the revolution**. Universities played a <u>significant role</u> in this movement as hubs of intellectual debates and protests.

> Young activists took to the streets in protest.

Students *Ahmad Ghandchi, Shariat-Razavi,* and *Bozorg-Ni…* were killed when the Shah's police fired on striking students at

Tehran University during US *Vice President Nixon*'s visit in 1953. Their **deaths sparked further activism** among Iran's youth, Islamic groups, and other activists.

From the outset, the Khomeini regime understood that Iran's **youth were crucial allies** in maintaining its rule. The regime updated textbooks to <u>focus on Islam</u> through Khomeini's perspective, reducing the history of Persian emperors and adding more about the ousting of the Pahlavi dynasty. And, during the Iran-Iraq War of the 1980s, the regime purposefully **enlisted young volunteers**, primarily from poor and rural backgrounds, to fight on the front lines. These youth were <u>urged to be loyal</u> to Khomeini and later used to enforce state control, including **suppressing protests**.

Despite promising freedom after the Shah was ousted in 1979, Khomeini's government **cracked down on free speech** and tightened control over schools, media, and public behavior. Many **young activists were sidelined** or had to flee, but some continued to <u>fight for democracy</u> and human rights, even risking their lives. In spite of the challenges, the **spirit of resistance among Iran's youth remains strong today**.

KABUL STUDENT UPRISINGS DEFY SOVIET RULE

"Tal de Vee Zamunga Isteqlal" or "Long live our independence" echoed through the streets of Kabul, Afghanistan, as schoolgirl *Nahid Saaed* threw her schoolmate's headscarf at pro-Soviet Afghan soldiers **during a protest** in April 1980. "You did not defend your homeland against the Russians," she exclaimed.

"You support them, so ... leave our weapons to us to protect the freedom of our homeland."

Nahid and other girls from two high schools in Kabul, Afghanistan, were **part of large protests organized by students** in the city. The youth of Kabul were demanding freedom and the removal of Soviet troops as soon as possible, after the Soviet Union had **invaded their country** and appointed a **communist government**.

Earlier that year, **thousands of Kabul's residents had rallied** in reaction to <u>arrests and killings of civilians</u> by Soviet officers. Eventually, security forces began shooting at the peaceful protestors, and Soviet tanks were used to stop the demonstration. **Six hundred civilians lost their lives**.

Only several weeks later, after the **presentation of a new national flag**, hundreds of **students rebelled** in the heart of Kabul. Their activism peaked on April 29, with multiple actions by student protestors. Around **5,000 students marched** to the former presidential residence, known as the *People's Palace*, and confronted the Soviet soldiers at its gates. Student demonstrators from *Omar Shahid High School* and *Habibia High School* were <u>shot and killed</u> during protests.

On that same day, girls from *Soriya Senior High School* and *Rabia-e Balkhi High School* organized a big action where they marched with other students to *Kabul University*, shouting

"LIBERTY OR DEATH."

As the activists tried to depart, security stopped them with force. It was here, on the front line, that Nahid Saaed made her **powerful act of protest** against the pro-Soviet soldiers.

Many people were killed in Kabul, and 30 schools were shattered after the deaths of their students. In their mourning of the slain youth, **Nahid became a symbol of resistance**.

RYAN WHITE CHANGES THE FACE OF AIDS AWARENESS

Ryan White, from Kokomo, Indiana, was **just 13 when he fell seriously ill** in 1984. He was suffering from chronic night sweats, diarrhea, stomach cramps, and exhaustion; when he ran a fever of 104 degrees, his mom, Jeanne, rushed him to the hospital.

Ryan was diagnosed with AIDS, the late stage of HIV—a virus that attacks cells that support the immune system's ability to fight infection. As a hemophiliac—someone with a genetic blood condition that can result in severe bleeding from minor cuts and injuries and who needs regular transfusions of blood—Ryan had become **infected from contaminated blood**.

> HIV was unlikely to be transmitted through casual contact.

Doctors told Ryan he only had 3–6 months to live, but he was still determined to return to school. HIV was **unlikely to be transmitted through casual contact**, including handshakes or

...using public restrooms. Even so, some teachers, parents, and other students **falsely suggested Ryan might spread the disease** simply by handling the newspapers he delivered on his paper route. The superintendent at Western Middle School **would not support Ryan's return**, and he was forced to listen to his seventh-grade classes over the telephone.

Ryan went to court and **won a case that allowed him to return** to the classroom, but he was left feeling sad and lonely by other students, who **mocked and turned away from him out of ignorance and fear.** His school forced him to eat with disposable cutlery, use separate bathrooms, and stopped

him from participating in gym classes. Some families pulled their children from classes and sent them to other schools. **His family was also targeted,** with trespassers breaking windows at their home and cashiers refusing to touch their hands at the grocery store.

Although there were cruel people in their community, the Whites received support from other families who defended Ryan's right to attend school. His local paper, *The Kokomo Tribune*, offered their support despite threats. Ryan bravely **spoke out about the misinformation and bigotry** he had suffered and soon became a national face for HIV/AIDS. He helped inspire other youth to be allies during nationwide school visits and charity events. Ryan's talks focused on confronting prejudice and stigma by building public awareness and calling for

kindness and empathy.

After living five years longer than doctors had told him he would, Ryan died one month before he finished high school. Congress passed the *Ryan White Comprehensive AIDS*

Resource Emergency (CARE) Act in August 1990 to honor the difference Ryan made with his activism and legacy.

> Ryan bravely spoke out about the misinformation and bigotry he had suffered.

Over the past three decades, **$300 million has been raised for more than 170 children's hospitals** in support of Ryan's mission to give children a healthy future. By bringing awareness to the subject of HIV/AIDS and confronting stigma, Ryan changed the conversation and opened doors for others to share their stories, organize for healthcare equity, **and make a difference**.

NOTHING ABOUT US, WITHOUT US: DEAF STUDENTS ORGANIZE

On March 6, 1988, a protest erupted at *Gallaudet University* in Washington, DC, founded to educate deaf and hard-of-hearing people. A coalition of students, faculty, staff, and alumni **banded together to fight** the university's *Board of Trustees'* decision to appoint a hearing person as their seventh president instead of one of two deaf candidates.

Although Gallaudet, a university supported by the government but not run by it, had been a global leader and bilingual driver of education, justice, and connection for the Deaf community for over a century, there was a **lack of Deaf representation** within the faculty. When Gallaudet's board began searching for the institution's seventh president, they didn't have unified support for a deaf leader among board members, despite strong student advocacy for a president with lived experience. The students sought a

> candidate capable of championing the Deaf community

and pushing the university to new heights, with the goal to push open doors for more deaf people to **assume leadership roles** throughout the university.

The standoff began on March 1, when a passionate group within the *National Association of the Deaf* (NAD) held a rally with **over a thousand students** in attendance. Inspired by the momentum of the demonstration, other small protests cropped up on campus the next day to call for a deaf president so deaf students could feel **heard, understood, and represented**

The coalition earned global attention and backing from celebrities, politicians, deaf workers in labor unions, and international leaders. In a show of support, many **American Sign**

Language-to-English interpreters joined the protest by offering their skills to help amplify the cause and connect with the bilingual student community on their terms.

"DEAF IS NOT SILENT"

Marchers and demonstrators carrying signs with the words, **"Deaf President Now," "Deaf Is Not Silent,"** and **"We Still Have a Dream"** spoke to the press and blocked campus gates to deliver their four demands:

1. Select a *DEAF* president

2. The Chair of the Board of Trustees of the university *MUST RESIGN*

3. At least *51%* of the Board of Trustees *MUST BE DEAF*

4. *NO PUNISHMENT* for students, staff, or faculty protestors

Initially, the board **refused to meet** the protestors' demands. Then, student leaders known as the **Gallaudet Four,** *Bridgetta Bourne, Jerry Covell, Greg Hlibok,* and

Tim Rarus, along with their supporters, marched to the US Capitol about a mile and a half away in defiance.

"WE STILL HAVE A DREAM"

Unstoppable, the protestors remained dogged in their pursuit, and their **steadfast efforts paid off**. On March 13, 1988, after more than a week of tension and conflict, the board gave in to pressure and **agreed to the demands**. The protestors' victory led to the <u>historic appointment</u> of *I. King Jordan* as the first deaf president since the university was founded in 1864. He became a spokesperson for the rights, abilities, and access of people with disabilities, and the Gallaudet protests became **a model for future disability justice movements across the globe.**

VELVET REVOLUTION

On *International Students Day 1989*—just eight days after the fall of the Berlin Wall in Germany on November 9— Prague, the capital city of Czechoslovakia, became a battleground. Despite being seen as gentle like velvet, **peaceful demonstrators**, driven by a desire to transition away from communist rule like their German neighbors, faced violent attempts to suppress their demands. Undeterred by riot police and the government's hostility, Czech and Slovak youth **stood firm against injustice with mostly nonviolent civil disobedience**.

Initially organized before the Berlin Wall came down, the demonstration was intended to commemorate the 50th anniversary of a **crackdown on a student demonstration** in Nazi-occupied Prague during World War II. The students were still permitted to rally, but with a warning: avoid the city center. Despite the directive from officials, **thousands marched** from campus toward the heart of Prague, **inspired by impassioned speeches**. They were also coaxed there by a young secret police operative disguised as a student. The gathering swelled, occupying *Wenceslas Square*, as **police sought to break up the demonstration** under the cover of night. Amid the clashes, many were attacked and injured. Although communist secret agents tried to disrupt the movement with the staged death of another operative as a **ploy to arrest activists**, the marchers persisted.

After the rally, demonstrators **organized a resistance group** called the *Civic Forum*, making their dissent visible and powerful through protests, political art, media engagement, strikes, and large rallies. **Singers and poets** also played a pivotal role, including those living in exile in Western Europe after being persecuted in Czechoslovakia for

using their voices for change.

By the end of November, hundreds of thousands of citizens of all ages had joined the cause. The growing momentum made it increasingly difficult for those in power to impede **the shift away from communism**, ultimately leading to its collapse. In 1990, Czechoslovakia witnessed its **first free and open elections, marking the end of over 40 years of communist rule.**

CHINESE STUDENTS CAPTURE THE WORLD'S ATTENTION

In 1989, Chinese youth courageously demanded a voice in their nation's future. From April to June, **students in Beijing and across the country staged pro-democracy protests**, marking a pivotal moment in communist China. For weeks, the youth, gathered at *Beijing's Tiananmen*

Square, inspired rallies throughout China, advocating for democracy, free speech, economic justice, and press freedom.

On May 13, the activists started a hunger strike to pressure *Communist Party* leaders into holding talks, and their numbers swelled as others joined, inspired to champion the cause. This led to a million-strong protest supporting the hunger-striking students and calling for change. After authorities visited the demonstrations on May 19, the students concluded their hunger strike. Tragically, **officials enforced martial law, turning the streets into a war zone** for the unarmed protestors. Despite an official declaration in the media that troops would **not harm innocents**, especially youth, a battalion of troops was unleashed, firing guns and driving tanks. Countless protestors were **crushed by the tanks**, and soldiers **mercilessly shot** demonstrators. Others were **arrested, tortured, and killed**.

> The youth, gathered at Beijing's Tiananmen Square, inspired rallies throughout China.

"Tank Man," a 19-year-old student, gained worldwide recognition when an **image of him standing in front of tanks** after the carnage was published in multiple countries outside of China. Various theories surround his fate; **whether he was arrested and punished or killed remains unclear**.

The image of Tank Man and the various forms of artistic expression it has inspired symbolize the quest for democracy in China that lives on today. Tank Man, or *"Unknown Rebel,"* as he is also known, was recognized as one of *TIME* magazine's *100 Most Important People of the Century* in 1998.

The day after the violence in Tiananmen Square, musician *Cui Jian* stepped onto a temporary stage in front of thousands of his fellow protestors and sang two songs with a **red bandana tied over his eyes in an act of defiance** and a call for reform. Communist officials <u>outlawed concerts</u> soon after.

Jian said later,

> *"I covered my eyes with a red cloth to symbolize my feelings. The students were heroes. They needed me, and I needed them."*

Authorities soon targeted the *Beijing Students Autonomous Federation*, a student group helping to organize the protests. Officials in Beijing **published a list of the names** of 21 students responsible for the Tiananmen Square protests. *Wang Dan, Wu'er Kaixi,* and *Chai Ling,*

among the young leaders involved, became **key targets of the government**. Media incessantly broadcasted the protestors' names, images, and descriptions. Officials **documented arrests and televised them** as they punished and, at times, executed advocates following unjust trials. *Operation Yellow Bird*, a British/Hong Kong-supported group, helped seven students on the list escape from China to <u>protect them from harm.</u>

Since 1989, China's government has **banned its citizens from openly discussing or commemorating the events** at Tiananmen Square. Despite the regime's attempts to maintain silence, the Tiananmen protests are **an enduring inspiration for global liberation movements.**

GENDER JUSTICE FOR A NEW GENERATION

Young feminists in the 1990s initiated a new era, or **"wave,"** of gender justice, fighting for social, political, economic, and cultural equality for people of all genders. They broke free from solely relying on the limits of past tactics and tools and **embraced a more culture-driven approach to activism**, harnessing the power of new tactics and tools, including technology, securing funding, and grassroots organizing both online and offline.

Born in the aftermath of the civil rights movements of the 1960s and 1970s, the *Third Wave* was influenced by the second wave of feminists in the 1960s, who were known for the slogan

"THE PERSONAL IS POLITICAL."

This means that people's **personal experiences are linked** with political and social systems, choices, and/or their relationship **to power in a state, culture, or institution**.

In 1992, 22-year-old *Rebecca Walker*, daughter of second-wave feminist and womanist *Alice Walker*, coined the phrase **"Third Wave"** in an article for *Ms.* magazine, a feminist publication her mother also wrote for which was launched in 1972. In her writing, Rebecca was keen to establish that this wave of feminism was **revolutionary in its own right** and could allow the next generation of feminists to <u>set their terms</u> for what feminism looked like for them and their times.

> They ... embraced a more culture-driven approach to activism.

Leading figures of the Third Wave **grew up in a media-rich environment** during the 1960s and 1970s. Shaped by technology, economic access, and cultural and LGBTQIA+ diversity, <u>they benefited from earlier feminists'</u> political, cultural, and economic achievements. Still, they **critiqued and added their perspectives** on systems, policies, and culture that remained unjust.

They also aimed to broaden feminist ideas, embracing theories like **intersectionality**. *Kimberlé Crenshaw*, a law professor, created the term intersectionality to explain how different parts of a person's identity, such as **race, gender, and sexuality**, come together and shape their experiences. It helps us see how **all aspects of who people are** can affect their access to opportunities and privileges, and how they are affected by systems like laws and policies.

After college, Rebecca Walker and *Shannon Liss* founded the nonprofit *Third Wave Fund* (now the *Third Wave Foundation*) to **inspire young feminist activism and leadership**. Today, the Third Wave Foundation continues to fund gender liberation work.

SERBIAN YOUTH CHALLENGE ELECTION FRAUD

On November 19, 1996, in a dance of defiance against a rigged election, a squad of gutsy *Belgrade University* students emerged as the masters of dissent. With a passion for justice, creative intelligence, and cheeky slogans, young Serbian activists turned peaceful protest into a **global model for artful change**. Leaders from the University of Belgrade created *Otpor!* ("Resistance!" in Serbian). Within a few years, their **nonviolent resistance campaign** became a larger movement against Serbia's leadership.

Guided by their desire to create more unity, encourage peaceful civic activism, and use thoughtful planning to make change, Otpor! used its **iconic black-fist logo** and battle cry of **"Gotov Je,"** or **"He's Finished,"** to oppose *President Slobodan Milosevic*. The students made their voices heard with protests beginning in *Niš*, where many people came together to **call for justice** after the *Serbian government tried to cheat in local elections.*

Despite the president's resounding declaration that the opposition had lost on February 11, 1997, the protests continued until March 22, 1997. Protest organizers wanted everyone to know that the local election results (and the opposition's victory) were not being honored after Milosevic **unjustly annulled the results**.

After opposition parties and university students **protested peacefully**, they laid the groundwork for further uprisings in 1998. Musician and activist *Srdja Popovic* and other young leaders orchestrated a massive **"get-out-the-vote"** campaign aimed at youth, propelling Otpor!'s membership to 70,000 by the time of the federal elections in 2000. **First-time voters played a significant role** in Milosevic's electoral defeat by voting against him in these elections, with almost **90 percent of 18 to 29 year olds participating**. Their innovative methods of expression, including humorous protest stickers, wall stencils, leaflets, concerts, stamps onto paper money, and street theater, were instrumental in amplifying their voices.

Ultimately, these **student demonstrations spread across the country**. Belgrade, the capital, was the site of Serbia's largest protests, with **hundreds of thousands** participating. Otpor!'s role in toppling Milosevic from power through marches, clever humor, and other nonviolent tactics not only advanced democracy in Serbia but also left an indelible mark on the world stage. Their model **shaped the planning and methods** of other youth movements in Egypt, Georgia, Iran, and Ukraine, demonstrating the far-reaching **influence of their innovative approach**.

STUDENTS AND FARMWORKERS UNITE FOR JUSTICE

"We'd rather go hungry than eat sweatshop tacos!"

was the passionate chant of a caravan of student, labor, and clergy hunger-strikers who picketed the fast-food restaurant *Taco Bell*'s headquarters in 2003. They were pushing for **improved pay and working conditions** for farmworkers who supplied the fast-food company's tomatoes.

In 2000, a group of youth activists formed the *Student/Farmworker Alliance* to advocate for better conditions for farmworkers. They organized on campus and in their communities **to mobilize others** to end unsafe and abusive **"sweatshops in the fields"** and joined forces with the *Coalition of Immokalee Workers* (CIW) to support tomato industry workers in Florida.

Disturbed by abuses of these workers' rights, the Student/Farmworker Alliance took part in a **230-mile march** from Fort Myers to Orlando, Florida, as part of the CIW's campaign for

"Dignity, Dialogue, and a Fair Wage." During this march, students from various Florida colleges raised awareness of how access to cheap, healthy food is a **human right**, as well as the importance of producing food in an environmentally friendly way, under **safe and fair conditions** for workers.

Using **direct action tools**, the students collaborated with the CIW to **launch a boycott of Taco Bells** across the US. Youth aged 18 to 24 played a critical role in the movement, as they were Taco Bell's top customers.

As part of their **"Boot the Bell"** campaign, 22 high schools and colleges collected petitions at food courts, **refused to buy from Taco Bell restaurants**, stood vigil, and refused campus sponsorships between 2002 and 2005. Due to their unyielding dedication, the boycott was successful, and Taco Bell agreed to all the CIW's demands. It was part of **one of the most successful labor actions** ever seen in the United States.

The boycott in Florida sparked **nationwide campaigns**, and students continued to speak out against Taco Bell. The well-coordinated movement and partnership between the coalition members left the company **unable to sign new contracts without concerns about a backlash** from its large consumer base. Linking the movement for sustainable food with social justice, they organized on campus and in their communities.

The Student/Farmworker Alliance continues campaigning for fair food wages and conditions with its partners today. It also continues to advocate for **workers' freedom from harassment and discrimination.**

YOUTH AGAINST CENSORSHIP AND ABSTINENCE-ONLY SEX ED

At the dawn of the 2000s, *Shelby Knox*, a determined 14-year-old from Lubbock, Texas, **led a movement to improve sex education.** Raised in a *Southern Baptist* family in a conservative town, Shelby was involved with a church group that taught it was wrong to educate teens about preventing unintended pregnancies or sexually transmitted infections.

Concerned about misinformation among her friends and their ability to learn about protecting their health and safety, Shelby **questioned the effectiveness of "wait until marriage" education** when teen pregnancy rates and sexually transmitted infections were rising in her community.

Shelby and her allies recognized and challenged the limitations of her church and the local authorities' approach. They formed alliances with local and national groups, including *Planned Parenthood* and *Advocates for Youth*, and launched a grassroots campaign for a **more inclusive and informative sex education curriculum.** They amplified their message by organizing campaigns, protests, social media outreach, and interviews. Despite resistance from parents, local authorities, politicians, and church leaders, Shelby and her peers **continued to fight for detailed and accurate reproductive health education.**

Shelby questioned the effectiveness of "wait until marriage" education when teen pregnancy rates and sexually transmitted infections were rising in her community.

Shelby's battle for **medically accurate and complete sex education** in Lubbock was featured in the PBS documentary *The Education of Shelby Knox*. The film documents her journey as a young activist, **highlighting the importance of youth voices** in shaping public policy and promoting social justice. It showcases Shelby's transformation from participating in church groups that promoted purity culture to **working with national organizations** to fight for change locally and nationally.

Despite resistance ... Shelby ... continued to fight for detailed and accurate reproductive health education.

Shelby's example of <u>teenage leadership</u> shows that it's never too early to take a stand, make change, and use our voices to speak truth to power. **Her work as an organizer, activist, and movement leader continues today.**

TRANSKIDS PURPLE RAINBOW FOUNDATION

At 6 years old, *Jazz Jennings* became a **trailblazer for transgender visibility**. Making headlines on a special edition of the *20/20* TV show in 2007, the South Florida youth, born in 2000, shared her story with America on one of its most powerful media platforms.

Jazz and her parents had already faced discrimination because of Jazz's gender, so after her TV appearance, they started the *TransKids Purple Rainbow Foundation* (TKPRF), an organization dedicated to spreading the message that

"tolerance, acceptance, and unconditional love are a birthright for all trans kids."

Jazz continued to face discrimination through her early life, including a **five-year denial of access** to the girls' restroom in elementary school and **exclusion** from the girls' soccer team due to a state ban. Jazz was forced to compete on a boys' team. But Jazz and her family fought back, and a public battle led to the *United States Soccer Federation* (USSF) influencing Florida to overturn the ban, paving the way for **more inclusive policies** for young athletes nationwide.

> Jazz and her family fought back ... influencing Florida to overturn the ban.

Informed by Jazz's experience and that of other trans children in the US, the TKPRF continues its work in fostering societal change by **empowering families** to support transgender and gender nonconforming children. They advocate for fair treatment, education, and research to **ensure the well-being and equality of all trans youth**. The foundation also amplifies the work of other young activists while providing information to youth and their families about safe and accessible places **to find belonging and connection**.

Jazz remains a strong advocate for trans rights as a young adult. Today, she continues to use her voice, art, and platform to **raise awareness and promote understanding**, addressing bias and intolerance despite facing hardship. Her foundation also speaks out about the need for a federal law to **protect trans children against more than 500 anti-trans state bills** targeting youth that have cropped up since 2022. Jazz's children's book, *I Am Jazz*, remains one of America's most challenged, censored, and banned books.

APRIL 6 MOVEMENT

In the spring of 2008, a group of young Egyptians used a simple Facebook page to spark a **powerful wave of change** in Egypt. Supporting striking textile workers, the young activists mobilized their <u>online communities</u> against high food prices and low wages. What began as a social media page asking people to wear black and stay home for a day of protest **turned into an unexpected channel for change**.

Inspired by Otpor!'s nonviolent approach in Serbia, they adopted a fist symbol in their materials. Their discussions on Facebook were intense, covering concerns about **free speech, government corruption, and the economy**. Utilizing platforms like Facebook and Twitter, the **tech-savvy youth shared information**, rallied public support, and monitored police actions.

> Tech-savvy youth shared information, rallied public support, and monitored police actions.

The **movement gained momentum** during a worker uprising on April 6, 2008, resulting in four deaths and the arrest of 400 people, including one of the movement's leaders, *Esraa Rashid*, who spent over two weeks in jail. In the wake of her televised release, **she disowned her activism**, which caused uncertainty in the movement over what to do next—but still, the protests continued.

Ahmed Maher, one of the movement's most visible activists, took on the leadership after Esraa. Ahmed had **endured a 12-hour beating** after being arrested on *President Hosni Mubarak*'s 80th birthday during a botched protest. He secured his release by **duping the authorities** and providing them with a fake Facebook password.

The work persisted, gaining support from **human rights groups and political allies worldwide**. Their resilience planted the seeds for the *Arab Spring* uprisings across the Middle East and North Africa in 2011, which left a lasting mark on the region's history.

By January 2009, the movement had grown rapidly to **70,000 members**, including youth, students, and citizens from diverse backgrounds who hadn't been engaged in political issues before. Despite an Egyptian court banning the April 6 Movement in 2014, **the spirit of their activism lived on**.

LEADING THE CHARGE FOR CHANGE IN IRAN

"Give us our votes back," chanted a crowd of mostly young Iranians who were dressed in green or holding green items like balloons. Feeling frustrated by their concerns about **rigged elections** in 2009, these protestors took over the capital Tehran's streets as **part of the political movement for peace and democracy** that was known as the "Green Wave."

GIVE US OUR VOTES BACK

Four years before, President Mahmoud Ahmadinejad's initial election had met widespread disapproval—especially among young people, including high school and college students, who **comprised 50% of the population under 30**. A movement opposing the new president arose peacefully but faced challenges as it grew and became more chaotic and violent. Ahmadinejad's **government led with aggression**, using batons and riot police to quash sit-ins and marches and arresting activists they viewed as enemies. Their methods stoked fear and inspired outrage.

The Green Movement began as a symbol for opposition leader Mir Hossein Mousavi's election campaign. It received its name from a green sash of support given to Mir Houssein Mousavi by Mohammad Khatami, Iran's former president and reformist leader. Up to **3 million peaceful protesters** filled Tehran's streets at the movement's height, challenging the official claim that Mahmoud Ahmadinejad had won the 2009 presidential election by a landslide. Their rallying cry was,

"Where is my vote?"

It later became a sign of hope and unity for people who **believed the election was unfair.** Many protestors displayed green symbols after being inspired by social media and blog posts to **stand against the rise of youth unemployment, gender inequality, and voter fraud.**

The re-elected President Ahmadinejad's **human rights offenses and resistance to a more open democracy** let down many young people who desired more freedom and protection. Since 2005, under his rule, **executions**—including those involving youth—**increased**. Despite threats to their safety and attempts by the government to silence rebellion, youth inspired by the Green Movement **engaged in civil disobedience** while also turning to art, music, filmmaking, and theater as a haven for connection, community building, and expression.

By the 2013 presidential election in Iran, the impact of the Green Movement was **still visible and impactful**. A shimmer of hope glimmered for young people seeking a brighter future beyond the shadows of arrests and brutality. Former diplomat and Islamic cleric *Hassan Rouhani* resonated more with Iran's youngest citizens due to his promise to deal with the nuclear crisis and repair troubled international relationships made worse under Ahmadinejad. The Green Movement had **engaged more young people** in the election process, which played a significant role in securing Rouhani's win.

THE ARAB SPRING

In the chill winds of December 2010, a groundswell of protest movements spread across Arab countries, starting in Tunisia. *Mohamed Bouazizi*, a street vendor, set himself on fire due to his anguish about his dire financial situation and experience with harassment by governing officials. His heartbreaking death <u>triggered outrage</u> about economic inequality and government corruption—frustrations felt by many in the neighboring countries. Soon, a wave of *"Arab Spring"* **protests against authoritarian governments swept the region, led mainly by young people** seeking dignity, liberty, human rights, and justice.

In 2011, protests erupted in Yemen, calling for change and *President Ali Abdullah Saleh*'s resignation. Yemen, one of the poorest nations in the Middle East, faced rising hunger due to **high food costs and fuel shortages**. Among the courageous voices against these conditions was *Hend Nasiri*, a 21-year-old Yemeni activist who founded youth organizations **advocating for women's rights and educational justice**. She said,

"The revolution is driven by the youth,"

describing how the young activists' on-the-ground and social media engagement **inspired others to get involved and advocate for human rights**.

Their efforts **moved and organized people** in Tunisia, Egypt, Libya, Syria, and elsewhere, demanding accountability and change. The ousting of Tunisia's *President Zine al-Abidine Ben Ali* was a historic event, while Egypt's *President Hosni Mubarak* resigned after protests.

But the path to change remained challenging. In Libya, the uprising against *Muammar-al-Qaddafi* turned into a **civil war with devastating consequences**. Syria faced a similar fate, as *President Bashar al-Assad* responded to protests with violence, plunging the nation into conflict.

Ten years later, **the Arab Spring's legacy remains complex**. While progress has been made in some areas, many difficulties persist. The region grapples with political instability, economic uncertainty, and social unrest. Yet the spirit of resilience and commitment to democracy and justice lives on as **young people speak out and fight for a brighter future**.

The spirit of resilience and commitment to democracy and justice lives on.

UK STUDENTS USE THEIR VOICE

"Stuff your cuts, we won't pay!" read a placard at a huge protest organized by the *National Campaign Against Fees and Cuts*. The march, which also saw rowdy clashes with police, had **drawn around 52,000 peaceful protestors** to London, England, on November 10, 2010. Their number included high school and university students from different backgrounds, workers, and even members of Parliament—all there **to campaign against increases in university tuition fees and budget cuts to public services**.

> Education should be available to everyone, regardless of income or class.

The government had examined the money spent on higher education in the wake of the *Great Recession*, which had deeply negatively impacted the UK economy. A report suggested **removing the limit on how much a student should pay in tuition fees** for university, sparking discontent among students and advocates for economic justice. Tensions rose further when it was proposed that fees should triple to around **£9,000 per year ($14,000 in US dollars)**.

Adding fuel to the fire, the leader of the *Liberal Democrat* party, *Nick Clegg*, had made a **pre-election promise** to halt any fee increase. However, after the election resulted in a hung parliament, the Liberal Democrat and *Conservative* parties formed an unexpected coalition government, and the Liberal Democrats **failed to deliver on their tuition fee promise**. This **betrayal** deeply affected the students of that time, many of whom still distrust the Liberal Democrats today.

Stressed about the escalating cost of education, students took to the streets of Central London in huge numbers, voicing their frustration over how the cuts and added debt would impact their education and later lives. When the government **went ahead with the increased fees**, more youth were inspired to join student movements. Public debates were sparked on how **education should be available to everyone, regardless of income or class**, and the students' education activism started broader conversations about how reductions in public spending affect healthcare and other basic human needs.

Organizations like *Defend the Right to Protest* and *Green and Black Cross* were also born from the 2010 movement. They provided legal support at demonstrations and transformed how activists in the UK access legal assistance. Some of these activists supported later movements like *Extinction Rebellion* and *Black Lives Matter*, representing the **power of collective action and how youth can bring about change.**

STUFF YOUR CUTS, WE WON'T PAY!

TEXAS STUDENTS PROTEST DEATH PENALTY

> "We're just ... being a voice for the voiceless,"

said *Rose Caldwell*, a university student and co-organizer of a landmark event to **protest the death penalty** in the United States. The event, held in San Antonio, Texas, was part of the movement in Rose's home state to ban lawmakers from **sentencing someone to die** for a crime if they are found guilty. Rose and her fellow protestors were determined to speak up for those who could no longer raise their voices because of the brutality of the death penalty.

Many San Antonio-area college students like Rose were inspired to ramp up their organizing after attending a leadership conference with the *Texas Coalition to Abolish the Death Penalty* (TCADP). The students' commitment

to advocacy grew with their growing influence, leading to the *Annual March to Abolish the Death Penalty* and the *Anti-Death Penalty Alternative Spring Break*, which allowed students to raise awareness and **act against the practice and policy**.

At these events, students from *St. Mary's University*, *Trinity University*, and other local colleges held signs and played protest songs about peace and justice from the *Civil Rights Movement* era. They spoke the names and stories of those **executed on death row** and read out the final goodbyes and pleas for action from inmates executed in Texas. Some **activists lay on the ground**, holding white paper crosses with the names of executed individuals.

Rose and her fellow protesters were determined to speak up for those who could no longer raise their voices because of the brutality of the death penalty.

The impact of the **passionate collective plea for justice** from Texas college students resonates in corridors of power across America and inspires others to join the fight. Over a decade later, the **death penalty is still practiced in more than 55 countries**, and student leaders are still actively fighting for reform.

OCCUPY MOVEMENT

"We are the 99%." was the rallying cry for the populist *Occupy* movement. It began in 2011, when a 28-year-old activist named *Chris* and his partner *Priscilla Grim* created a *Tumblr* blog highlighting how the vast majority of people were struggling economically (the **99%**), while a wealthy elite held most of the world's wealth (the **1%**). Their blog **brought attention to the issues** of fairness and responsibility in big business, finance, corporate law, and banking. By asking users (including many young people) to share their stories on a sign, then take a selfie and upload it to the page, the Tumblr encouraged **unity between working people and supporters of economic justice**.

"WE ARE THE 99%"

Each story shared how financial challenges like wage inequality, student debt, and healthcare affected people's lives, sometimes for generations. Described by some as online bathroom graffiti, this platform **created a path for connections**, fostering a sense of unity and solidarity. Most of all, it helped motivate people to demand an end to excess and greed in finance and business and **a closing of the vast economic gap** between the wealthy and working people struggling to make ends meet.

Meanwhile, *Kalle Lasn*, who cofounded *Adbusters* magazine, was **advocating the same issues** as Chris and Priscilla.

In collaboration with *Adbusters* senior editor, *Micah White*, he planned a protest in Lower Manhatten, New York. Inspired by the success of the *Egyptian Revolution* demonstrations, Lasn and White planned a tent city **"occupation"** of Wall Street, where many banks and other financial organizations have their headquarters. Lasn started the *OccupyWallStreet.org* website and selected September 17 for people to act against <u>corporate greed</u> and excess. *Facebook* and *Twitter* were abuzz in the lead-up, although behind closed doors, some organizers known as the *New York General Assembly* were **worried the plan might flop** because there weren't enough people to stage a big enough protest.

> It helped motivate people to demand an end to excess and greed in finance and business.

However, the **Occupy tent-city movement grew swiftly,** and tent-driven protests spread to other cities worldwide. *Occupy Wall Street*'s tent city thrived for 59 days with the eyes of the <u>world watching on livestream</u> until *Mayor Bloomberg*'s police force swept the campsite. Despite removing this physical site of action, it sparked a global movement of Occupy actions on and offline, including *Occupy London* and *Occupy Lisbon*, *RIP Medical Debt*. "Occupy"-inspired actions and tent encampments are **still being used as a tactic in environmental justice and anti-war student protest movements** today.

EGYPT'S YOUTH SHAPE THE REVOLUTION

A baby girl was named **"Facebook"** by her father, *Jamal Ibrahim,* in honor of *Facebook*'s role in organizing Egypt's 18-day protest in early 2011. In January that year, **protests had surged, led by young activists demanding democracy and free elections**. Building on the momentum of the April 6 Movement from 2008, Egyptians united to call for *President Mubarak*'s immediate resignation.

Social media played a crucial role, with Google employee *Wael Ghonim*'s **"We are all Khaled Said"** Facebook page igniting change. The page was created after 28-year-old *Khaled Said* was brutally beaten to death by plainclothes Egyptian police. Images of his death spread online, **fueling outrage** over poverty, police brutality, youth unemployment, and government corruption.

"WE ARE ALL KHALED SAID"

The tragedy of Khaled Said and dissatisfaction with Egypt's government **ignited widespread protests**, particularly in Cairo's Tahrir Square. As the protests grew in January 2011,

Building on the momentum of the April 6 Movement from 2008, Egyptians united to call for President Mubarak's immediate resignation.

Mubarak's government cut off internet access, blocked social media, and used violence to stop the demonstrators. **Despite these efforts, the unrest continued.**

Mubarak attempted to quell the protests by promising his future resignation and proposing a new vice president. However, the protests persisted for nearly three weeks, leading to **Mubarak's resignation and the military's takeover**, ending his 30-year rule.

Although the protests didn't immediately result in the democracy and free elections the protesters sought, the **pro-democracy wave also swept through several Middle East and North African countries**, including Bahrain, Oman, Jordan, Morocco, and Algeria.

STUDENT STRIKERS CAMPAIGN TO CANCEL STUDENT DEBT

One day in 2014, around 2,700 Americans opened their mail to find a surprising letter from the *Rolling Jubilee* initiative. For some people, **it was a life-changing moment.** These Americans were in debt, some for tens of thousands of dollars because they wanted a college education to improve their career opportunities. The letter from Rolling Jubilee said they would be **removing some of that debt, thanks to the work of activists** who believed everyone should have fair access to education without the burden of stifling debt.

During his campaign in the late 1960s, *Governor Ronald Reagan* of California attacked public education funding. He pushed for increasing college tuition charges, arguing that the state **"should not subsidize intellectual curiosity."** Reagan criticized the student protesters involved in the *Free Speech Movement* at Berkeley, calling them **"spoiled"** and claiming they **"don't deserve the education they are getting."**

> Everyone should have fair access to education without the burden of stifling debt.

Reagan's victory led other elected officials in New York and Florida to **cut public funding for higher education**. This trend spread throughout the United States. With higher tuition costs, students had to **take out loans from banks to pay for their education**, leaving them with <u>burdensome debt</u> that affected their healthcare, family planning, and economic decisions.

In 2012, the *Debt Collective* was formed, calling themselves **"debt resisters."** They created a manual explaining systems and actionable tools, spread awareness using

protest art, and launched their Rolling Jubilee initiative. The **initiative crowdfunded to buy millions of dollars of debt** from lenders who no longer wanted to chase that debt for repayment. Normally, people who bought debt from lenders would then demand repayment themselves, but Rolling Jubilee **canceled it as an act of protest**. They canceled <u>over $32 million</u> in medical, student, payday loan, and probation debt. Their efforts **inspired more activists** to push politicians for fairer policies for student borrowers.

The debate continues in the United States over whether it's an individual student's choice and responsibility to pay for their college education, or whether having a greater number of college-educated people benefits the wider public and should therefore be supported by public money. The *Supreme Court* ruled against student debt cancellation in 2023, but *President Joe Biden*'s administration found other ways to <u>cancel $48 billion</u> of student debt. Even so, around 43 million Americans continue to carry education debt, and **activists and allies continue to push for cancellation and affordable education for all.**

DREAM DEFENDERS

"We are a movement of a new generation ... We are an organized youth resistance,"

said the *Dream Defenders*, a youth-led movement of Black, Arab, and Latinx activists, whose 2013 sit-in at the Florida State Capitol lasted for 30 nights and 31 days. They were **fighting to end racial profiling and repeal /tand Your Ground laws.**

The early seeds of the movement's work were planted in the spring of 2006, when Florida students *Ramon Alexander, Phillip Agnew, Gabriel Pendas*, and *Ahmad Abuznaid* (joined by other students and supporters), protested the lack of an **investigation into the death** of *Martin Lee Anderson*, a 14-year-old Black teenager who died in a violent juvenile boot camp. Their experiences in **organizing peaceful protests** laid the groundwork for their future activism.

But it was almost six years later, after the killing of *Trayvon Martin*, an unarmed 17-year-old Black teenager in Florida, by vigilante shooter *George Zimmerman* on February 26, 2012, that the Dream Defenders was born. After a **call to action was shared** on Facebook, young activists marched from Daytona Beach to Sanford, the location of Trayvon's killing, to demand

Zimmerman's arrest. Phillip, Ahmad,and Gabriel, alongside Florida A&M students *Nelini Stamp* and *Ciara Taylor*, cofounded the movement, focusing on **nonviolent civil disobedience and direct-action organizing.**

> "They were fighting to end racial profiling and repeal Stand Your Ground laws."

The Dream Defenders' sit-in at the Florida Capitol occurred alongside nationwide protests against the release of George Zimmerman on "self-defense" grounds. The release highlighted **injustices within the criminal justice system**. Social media and partnerships with other groups nationwide amplified their cause, leading to increased support.

Today, the Dream Defenders continue to advocate for justice and equality.

MALALA ADVOCATES FOR GIRLS' EDUCATION

In 1997, a baby girl named *Malala Yousafzai* was born in the Swat Valley of Pakistan. Her family valued education highly, and her father, *Ziauddin Yousafzai*, ran a school and encouraged Malala's **love for learning**. After the *Taliban* took control of the region in 2007 and **imposed strict laws, including a ban on girls' education**, their lives changed dramatically.

Despite the Taliban's oppressive rule and facing threats, Malala remained **determined to pursue education** and speak out against injustice. She contributed to a global blog under a pseudonym, sharing her experiences and **advocating for girls' right to learn.**

> Malala remained determined to pursue education and speak out against injustice.

In 2012, the Taliban, feeling **threatened by her influence, attempted to kill Malala.** A gunman shot her in the head while she was on her way home from school. Miraculously, **Malala survived** and was flown to the United Kingdom for emergency medical treatment.

Malala underwent numerous surgeries and a long recovery but **remained dedicated to advocating for girls' education.** Her story captured global attention and **garnered widespread support.**

In 2014, Malala became the youngest recipient of the prestigious *Nobel Peace Prize* at 17, recognized for her tearless

She works tirelessly to ensure every girl has access to quality education.

advocacy for children's rights. She continued her education at Oxford University, studying philosophy, politics, and economics. Today, Malala is a **prominent advocate** for education and girls' rights worldwide. Through her organization, the *Malala Fund*, she works tirelessly to ensure **every girl has access to quality education**, pushing for policy changes that prioritize education for girls and young women.

> "One child, one teacher,
> one book, one pen
> can change the world."

As Malala famously said, "One child, one teacher, one book, one pen can change the world." Her journey from a young girl standing up for her education to an international symbol of courage and resilience shows how powerful it can be to raise your voice and fight for your beliefs. Her unwavering determination demonstrates that **positive change can be achieved through bravery and perseverance**, even in adversity.

YOUTH ADVANCE RACIAL JUSTICE AND "BUILD BLACK FUTURES"

In February 2012, *Trayvon Martin*, a 17-year-old, was at his father's home in Florida when he became hungry for snacks. So Trayvon walked to a nearby *7-Eleven* store. But on his way back, Trayvon, an unarmed Black youth, was shot by *George Zimmerman* in a **brutal act of vigilante violence**. Trayvon's killing **sparked national outrage**, leading to protests, marches, and petitions.

> They ... demanded an end to inequity and racial profiling, which targets people based on bias and stereotypes.

The Million Hoodies for Trayvon **movement emerged** when youth organized massive protests seeking justice for *Trayvon Martin*, who was wearing a hoodie when he was shot. People marched in their own hoodies and demanded **an end to inequity and racial profiling**, which targets people based on bias and stereotypes. This pivotal moment roused next-generation youth, who were horrified that such **violence driven by harmful stereotypes** led to this tragic and unjust loss of an innocent life.

As the protests grew, three women emerged as key figures in the global fight for justice: *Alicia Garza*, *Patrisse Cullors*, and *Opal Tometi*. In July 2013, following Zimmerman's acquittal, Patrisse used the hashtag *#BlackLivesMatter* in a social media post, **birthing a movement that changed history**. It was an affirmation, a love letter to their community, a bearing of witness, and **a call to action**.

Between 2013 and 2014, #BlackLivesMatter continued to expand, highlighting cases of **anti-Black racism and police brutality** and advocating against it. Protests spread from Ferguson, Missouri, to New York City, fueled by the deaths of *Michael Brown, Eric Garner, Tamir Rice, Sandra Bland,* and other Black people killed by police and vigilantes.

In 2013, *Cathy Cohen* and *Charlene Carruthers* launched *Black Youth Project 100* (BYP100) as a dynamic movement for young Black activists to **mobilize their community for social justice**. During an initial BYP meeting, the verdict in the Trayvon Martin case was announced, releasing George Zimmerman from guilt. Tears flowed, and cries pierced the air as a mix of outrage, grief, despair, and determination transformed into action. **From this moment, BYP100 deepened its engagement in grassroots activism.**

In Ferguson, Missouri, unrest followed the fatal shooting of 18-year-old Michael Brown by police officer *Darren Wilson.* The unrest from August 9 to 25, 2014, and again in later periods, **underscored racial justice issues**. The *Department of Justice* examined the Ferguson police department's practices, **revealing patterns of discrimination**.

#BlackLivesMatter ... was an affirmation, a love letter to their community, a bearing of witness, and a call to action.

And the following month, *Darnell Moore* and Patrisse Cullors organized the *Black Life Matters Ride* to Ferguson. Over 600 participants traveled there to support Ferguson's community and **address systemic racism nationwide**. The movement recognized Ferguson as a **symbol** of broader injustices and gave organizers a framework for activism they could apply in their communities.

"BUILD BLACK FUTURES"

But it was after the murders of *Ahmaud Arbery* in Georgia, *George Floyd* in Minnesota, and *Breonna Taylor* in Kentucky in 2020 that momentum ramped up for the *Movement for Black Lives*, also known as #BlackLivesMatter or #BLM in public conversation and online. An **unprecedented wave of protests** across the United States and worldwide moved **70% of young Americans age 11 to 15** to engage with the BLM movement through marches, walkouts, social media activism, and creating protest art.

BLM, led by a board of directors, is now a network of local chapters. BYP100 also **remains active**, aiming to "build Black futures."

#1000BLACKGIRL BOOKS

After becoming frustrated with the lack of Black characters in the books available in her fifth-grade classroom, 11-year-old *Marley Dias* took action. She **collected and distributed 1,000 books featuring Black girls** as main characters to other young readers, launching her campaign, *#1000BlackGirlBooks*. This initiative helped young readers see themselves reflected in stories, in a media and publishing landscape that often lacked representation of their local and global communities. Marley **enabled diverse readers to connect with their stories** and experiences by promoting Black girls and their voices.

WE NEED DIVERSE BOOKS

In 2015, the literary world saw a shift with the *We Need Diverse Books* movement, which emphasized the importance of diversity in all its aspects. This movement connected with Marley's campaign, further highlighting the need for representation. Soon after, the *#ownvoices* movement gained momentum, **empowering authors to share their stories authentically** through their lived experiences.

> Marley enabled diverse readers to connect with their stories and experiences by promoting Black girls and their voices.

Throughout her teens, Marley **continued her activism**. She wrote and contributed to articles, essays, and books, sharing her story and encouraging other young people to advocate for change in their communities. Marley's efforts raised awareness and **laid important groundwork** for the ongoing movement to create a **more inclusive literary world** for readers of all ages. We Need Diverse Books, #ownvoices, and #1000BlackGirlBooks collectively made a difference by fostering this inclusivity.

In 2020, Marley hosted her first Netflix show, **Bookmarks: Celebrating Black Voices,** which shares Black stories and inspires young people to read.

STUDENTS TAKE ON UNFAIR DRESS CODES

In 2015, *Maggie Sunseri*, a junior in high school from Versailles, Kentucky, made a documentary and shared it on YouTube. Observing how **girls were treated differently from boys** in the enforcement of her school's dress code, Maggie filmed *Shame: A Documentary on School Dress Code* and began a **peaceful yet powerful rebellion against bias in schools** based on gender and identity stereotypes.

In Maggie's school, there was an **outdated belief** that girls wearing certain clothing would distract boys, so she decided to shed light on how these **dress code policies affected girls' self-esteem and confidence**. Her film spurred dress-code activism on social media platforms as **students nationwide**

protested, petitioned, and walked out of school to challenge discriminatory dress codes in their communities. Their number included *Anna Loisa Cruz* from Portland, Oregon, who shared a story about a schoolmate sent home for a slightly short skirt, and *Hailey Tjensvold*, who highlighted the **different consequences for boys** with sagging pants compared to girls facing scrutiny for attire deemed "revealing."

Recognizing the need to respect diverse student identities, the battle against dress codes is **not merely about clothing or personal presentation**. The movement remains a fight against control and pressure based on how people look instead of who they are, inspiring youth from marginalized cultures and religions, gender nonconforming students, and transgender students to organize for **more inclusive dress code standards**.

> There was an outdated belief that girls wearing certain clothing would distract boys.

The fight for freedom of expression in schools continues to this day. At *Barbers Hill High School* in Texas, 18-year-old *Darryl George* was **disciplined for refusing to cut his locs** multiple times between 2023 and 2024. School officials argued that his hair was too long, even though the *CROWN Act* protects hairstyles such as locs, twists, or braids from discrimination.

YOUNG WATER PROTECTORS' PIPELINE PROTEST

At 9 years old, *Tokata Iron Eyes*, a member of the *Standing Rock Sioux Tribe* of North Dakota, testified against a mine that would **harm the sacred land** on their reservation. They continued to be immersed in activism as they grew older, and at the age of 12, became a *Water Protector* as part of the campaign against the *Dakota Access Pipeline* (DAPL) in 2016. Water Protectors are activists committed to safeguarding water sources from contamination and **preserving Indigenous lands and rights.**

"WATER IS LIFE"

The struggle against the pipeline began in 2016 on the sweeping plains of the *Standing Rock Sioux Reservation*. The Dakota Access Pipeline (DAPL) was planned to transport oil but **threatened the ancestral lands** of the Indigenous people and risked contaminating the Missouri River—the lifeline of the Reservation. This caused outrage among Indigenous communities and environmentalists, sparking a fierce **global resistance movement**.

Indigenous people from many groups set up camp near the Missouri River, where the DAPL was planned to cross. Wood for campfires was scarce on the Great Plains, so **activists and their allies sent firewood to warm the protestors** in the biting cold. Supporters brought it to the camp, along with protective clothes, food, and horse tack for Sioux youth riders.

> The Dakota Access Pipeline (DAPL) ... risked contaminating the Missouri River—the lifeline of the Reservation.

PROTECT OUR WATER
#NO DAPL

FOR
FUTURE
GENERATIONS

By 2017, tensions were
mounting, and young
activists, including
Jasilyn Charger, joined
forces with Iron Eyes and
the Standing Rock Water
Protectors. They stood together to **defend the rights of Indigenous people as custodians of the land** and to protect the environment, transcending borders from Canada to the United States. These Water Protectors marched and stood strong at the pipeline standoff with signs saying, **"Protect Our Water, #NoDAPL," "For Future Generations,"** and **"Water is Life."**

They stood together to defend the
rights of Indigenous people ... and to
protect the environment.

From the heart of Standing Rock, Tokata Iron Eyes continued their advocacy journey. In September 2019, they crossed paths with renowned Swedish activist and *School Climate Strike* founder *Greta Thunberg*. The pair teamed up to organize rallies and events in North Dakota and South Dakota, including an appearance at *Standing Rock High School*. Now at the forefront of the international climate justice movement, Iron Eyes continues to **amplify Indigenous voices and confront environmental injustices worldwide**, showing how global struggles over land and climate justice are deeply connected.

BANA AL-ABED BEARS WITNESS

"I need peace."

Seven-year-old Syrian *Bana al-Abed*'s short tweet about the siege of her hometown, Aleppo, in September 2016 **created ripples of awareness across the globe**. Bana's Twitter account was created by her English-teacher mother, *Fatemah*, and became well-known worldwide after she shared her firsthand experiences online during the ongoing **Syrian civil war**.

Bana often used # Aleppo in her tweets to draw attention to the **human cost of the Syrian conflict**. Her thoughts and fears about her daily life, including tweets such as "I hate war" and "And the world has forgotten us," built awareness and **moved onlookers to speak up and act**.

Amid the ruins of her home, Bana used her Twitter platform to **document her family's harrowing escape** from Eastern Aleppo's destruction by the Syrian Army. She expressed a deep yearning for her lost home and **pleas for peace** while painting a vivid picture of hunger, airstrikes, and the bombing of her school and garden.

When Bana's Twitter activity stopped, hundreds of thousands of <u>worried followers</u> used the hashtag **#WhereIsBana** to find her. As her Twitter community grew increasingly disturbed by Bana's silence, *Harry Potter* author *J. K. Rowling* revealed her knowledge that Bana was still alive. Rowling shared that **they had been in touch online** when she sent Bana a *Harry Potter* ebook after **receiving a message** from the young storyteller.

"THE WORLD HAS FORGOTTEN US"

Soon after, **Bana's home was bombed again**. She and her family survived, but with injuries, and Bana's parents decided the time had come to <u>escape Syria.</u> The family found refuge in Turkey, where Bana continued her activism, sharing films of herself with homemade signs calling for an end to the bombing. Her efforts **gained increased international attention**, leading her to meet with world leaders and be mentioned at the *United Nations*.

Today, Bana is the **author of multiple books** about her experience, including *Dear World*. She is now a Turkish citizen who told media outlets that **her dream is to grow up and become a teacher in Aleppo like her mother**.

LITTLE MISS FLINT TACKLES THE WATER CRISIS

In 2016, 8-year-old *Amariyanna "Mari" Copeny*, a resident of Flint, Michigan, wrote a letter to *President Barack Obama* to highlight the **water pollution disaster that had been happening in her city** for about two years.

Mari's heartfelt letter asking for the president's help revealed the grim reality that thousands of people in Flint were **forced to drink and bathe in brown, foul-smelling water**. The water was so loaded with <u>chlorine disinfectant</u> to remove microorganisms and other potentially harmful diseases that it damaged new engine parts at a local plant.

Mari's letter, written with urgency, **requested a meeting with the president** for herself and other community members when they traveled to the capital to witness their governor testify before Congress about the water disaster. But Mari's words **moved the president so deeply**, he invited her to meet with him during his trip to Flint and arranged **to invest $100 Million** to address the crisis.

Mari's letter and meeting with President Obama **inspired wide-reaching support** for her cause. Her personal experiences and those of her community, many of whom had experienced financial difficulties and neglect by state officials, fed her passion for justice and government responsibility. Mari became a **powerful advocate** against economic injustice and environmental racism.

Mari's commitment to her cause is unwavering. She continues to address the wider US clean-water crisis and other social justice causes on social media, using her platform to **amplify the voices of those affected**. On X, she boldly stated,

"Flint is just one city out of hundreds. I've been screaming America has a water crisis for almost 5 years."

And, as a youth ambassador for the *2017 Women's March*, she **raised significant funds** for essentials like school supplies, toys, bottled water, books, and clean filters, demonstrating her ongoing dedication to supporting her community.

In addition to her quest for clean water and raising funds for disadvantaged communities, Mari **uplifts young voices** and actively works to build a healthier future for the next generation. A presidential hopeful for 2044, Mari Copeny has already put her stake in the ground for **her campaign to advance change in America now and into the future.**

"NEVER AGAIN": YOUTH DEMAND GUN CONTROL

> "Enough with 'thoughts and prayers'—students demand action!"

This rallying cry echoed across America as brave students united in the wake of devastating shootings of students and school staff, determined to **fight for safer schools, stronger gun laws, and fairness for all**. They refused to stay silent in the face of challenges, pushing back against the empty promises of pro-gun lawmakers.

Student-led activism gained momentum after a horrific massacre at *Marjory Stoneman Douglas High School* in Parkland, Florida, on February 14, 2018. Survivors *X González* and *David Hogg* turned their grief into action, joining forces with students nationwide. On March 24, 2018, **over a million people** gathered at the *March for Our Lives* in Washington, DC, and other events across the country to support the

They refused to stay silent ... pushing back against the empty promises of pro-gun lawmakers.

students' **call for stricter gun control laws.** *Naomi Wadler,* an inspiring young activist, staged a walkout at *George Mason Elementary School* with 60 classmates, and *Never Again MSD,* a political action group, was formed by students from Marjory Stoneman Douglas High School to push for stricter gun control. Their advocacy became widely known for the hashtags **#NeverAgain** and **#EnoughIsEnough**.

After a horrific shooting on March 27, 2023, at *The Covenant School* in Nashville, Tennessee, high school and college students nationwide took to the streets, **calling for gun safety measures**. An ex-student shot and killed three children and three adults at the elementary school, sparking renewed demands for gun control.

#NEVERAGAIN

On March 30, Tennessee Democratic Reps. *Justin Jones, Gloria Johnson,* and *Justin Pearson,* known as the **"Tennessee Three,"** were expelled by Republican officials for participating in a **gun control protest on the House floor**. The decision drew cries of **"shame on you"** during the proceedings as Rep. Johnson, a white woman in her sixties, **was not censured**, while Jones and Pearson, young Black lawmakers, **were ousted**. This sparked a strong backlash against their removal and a victorious grassroots campaign to re-elect **"The Justins."**

#ENOUGHISENOUGH

Over **300 walkouts** took place **across 40 states and Washington, DC,** as youth organizers and their parents demanded change beyond the **"thoughts and prayers"**

> Protestors highlighted a link between race and hate crimes in the wake of school shootings.

statements that were usual from pro-gun lawmakers following mass shootings. These demonstrations were co-organized by *Everytown Against Gun Violence*, *Students Demand Action*, and their coalition, increasing **pressure on the gun industry** for their role in making schools and students unsafe.

The movement also extended beyond gun violence, as protestors highlighted a link between race and hate crimes in the wake of school shootings. In Missouri, less than a month after the Covenant School shooting, Black teenager *Ralph Yarl* was shot by 84-year-old *Andrew Lester* for ringing the wrong doorbell while trying to pick up his siblings. Lester's violent attack on the unarmed Yarl inspired an outcry about the role of targeted racism in gun violence. Lester's grandson, *Klint Ludwig*, was not surprised, saying, "I believe he held-holds-racist tendencies and beliefs." A thousand *Staley High School* students walked out to support their classmate during Lester's trial, **raising money for Yarl's cause and advocating for justice and equality**.

From a nationwide movement to localized actions, the collective voice and unflinching determination of **youth-led activism continues the urgent call** for legislative changes, school safety, gun control, and racial justice,

TEENS TAKE THE LEAD TO SAVE THE PLANET

In Stockholm, Sweden, *Greta Thunberg*, the daughter of an opera singer and an actor, became aware of the **urgency of climate change** when she was very young. Her distress over the grim state of the environment led her to a long period of selective mutism, a condition where she stopped speaking except with her family. But in 2018, age 15, she used her voice to become a bold **advocate for the planet**.

On August 20, 2018, Greta staged a solo protest outside the Swedish parliament, holding a sign that read "**Skolstrejk för klimatet**" (School Strike for Climate). This act sparked a global movement. Greta's sign motivated youth worldwide, who rallied under the "**Fridays for Future**" banner, demanding government accountability and **raising awareness about the climate crisis** through school strikes, walkouts, and marches. Greta's actions, including skipping school every Friday to **strike for 251 weeks** and her carbon-neutral boat journey across the Atlantic to attend the *UN Climate Action Summit*, amplified her climate justice message.

"FRIDAYS FOR FUTURE"

Greta's forceful and informed pleas to world leaders, including her **powerful speech** at the *United Nations*, earned her a nomination for the *Nobel Peace Prize 2019*. That same year, she won *TIME* magazine's *Person of the Year* award, making her the youngest recipient of this recognition. *Dr. Martin Luther King Jr.* had been named Person of the Year for 1963, highlighting the gravity of Greta's achievement.

> She used her voice to become a bold advocate for the planet.

When the *COVID-19* pandemic disrupted traditional in-person protests, young activists like Greta, *Disha Ravi* in India, and *Vanessa Nakate* in Uganda leaned more deeply into **online activism**. Greta shared her experience as a person on the autistic spectrum on Instagram in 2019, saying,

"I'm sometimes a bit different from the norm. And—given the right circumstances—being different is a superpower."

Despite facing challenges, online abuse, and backlash, including Disha's controversial arrest by Indian authorities, **these young advocates remained unwavering in their commitment to saving the planet**.

Greta's forceful and informed pleas to world leaders ... earned her a nomination for the Nobel Peace Prize 2019.

The global student climate strikers' collective efforts continue to inspire action and **hold leaders accountable for environmental stewardship**. In the ongoing fight for climate justice, these young revolutionaries and their courageous acts are helping shape **a sustainable future for the generations to come.**

GIRLS STAND UP FOR GLOBAL RIGHTS

On the *International Day of the Girl* 2019, six young women between 17 and 22 years old gathered at the United Nations in New York City. *Djellza Pulatani* from Kosovo, *Faith Nwando* from Nigeria, *Olivia Lombardo* from Italy, *Kanchan Amatya* from Nepal, *Vishakha Agrawal* from India, and *Angélica Morales* from Mexico were there to reveal the *Global Girls' Bill of Rights*, which would **universally declare the rights of girls around the world.**

A devoted group of young women spread across seven different time zones, including these six representatives, worked together using *WhatsApp* to create a historic proclamation that amplified the voices of **over 1,000 young women and girls from 34 countries.** With the support of international nonprofits *Akili Dada, She's the First*, and *MAIA Impact*, the document was delivered to *UN Women*, a department of the United Nations dedicated to **gender equality**, to announce their shared cause.

The Girls' Bill of Rights **demanded** that governments, lawmakers, organizations, and the world as a whole **support girls' fundamental rights to health, education, safety, and consent in relationships**. The activists raised their voices to support women living with discrimination, cultural inequality, violence, and poverty, promoting issues such as the inclusion of women in *STEM* fields, tackling the plight of missing and stolen girls, and *Chhaupadi*, an ancient Hindu tradition that banishes girls and young women into isolation during their period.

> Activists raised their voices to support women living with discrimination, cultural inequality, violence, and poverty.

As passionate advocates for the Bill, the six young women presented their findings and vision to the *Deputy Secretary-General of the United Nations* and documented their experiences through blogs and media interviews.

★ In a world where **one girl younger than 15 is married every seven seconds** and **130 million girls cannot attend school**, the Girls' Bill of Rights continues to be a unified call to hear and support girls worldwide and to put them **at the forefront of creating solutions** that affect their own lives.

EXTINCTION REBELLION YOUTH

Extinction Rebellion (XR) was launched in the UK in 2018 with a **mission to save the planet from environmental disaster**. The founding activists of XR burst onto the scene with a steadfast mission: to shake up governments and rescue the Earth. Known for their <u>bold tactics</u>, XR first captured the public's attention by "occupying" environmental charity *Greenpeace*'s London offices.

XR believed traditional methods of changemaking, such as petitioning, lobbying, and voting, were **limited due to the grim realities** of climate change and animal extinction. The group's tactics promoted a <u>sense of urgency</u>, arguing that individual choices cannot solve the problem **without changes in our systems and institutions**.

As XR protests continued, **more supporters joined**. Bridges and major roads were blocked, and protestors smashed windows, among other **acts of civil disobedience**.

Although their rebellions captured the public's attention, **reactions were mixed** due to the <u>impact on people</u> being blocked from accessing public spaces like airports or hospitals during health emergencies.

In February 2019, a youth branch of the movement formed. *Extinction Rebellion Youth* (XRY) emerged as an independent wing of XR **advocating for peaceful but swift action** on climate change, biodiversity loss, and other societal threats. As 19-year-old student XRY activist *Savannah Lovelock*, who forgoes flying for ethical reasons and **deferred university to focus on climate justice**, said,

> "We are consistently being punched in the face by the truth, but nobody is doing anything."

In Australia, XRY blocked a freeway in Melbourne to protest injustice, and participated in **nationwide rebellions** to stop Blak Indigenous deaths in police custody. In Brazil, they organized an **educational event** in Manaus to amplify the effects of the climate crisis and displayed a banner saying **"SOS AMAZONIA"** at the *Ministry of the Environment*, highlighting the urgent need to protect the Amazon rainforest from deforestation and exploitation. XRY also intentionally **prioritized inclusivity** and amplifying voices from communities in the Global South, emphasizing **the importance of listening to and supporting those most affected by climate change.**

Now with hundreds of branches globally, **XRY continues to inspire young leaders** to join the fight for a **sustainable future**.

FILIPINO YOUTH MOBILIZE FOR CLIMATE ACTION

In November 2013, the devastating *Typhoon Haiyan* hit the Philippines, causing widespread destruction. After around 8,000 people died and 4 million were displaced as a result of the storm, the catastrophic event highlighted the country's urgent need for climate justice. In response to the dangers of warming oceans that can cause more intense, unpredictable, unseasonal, and destructive storms, a **new generation of youth activists emerged,** driven by a shared determination **to address the root causes of such disasters.**

Teenager Mitzi Jonelle Tan from the Metro Manila area of the Philippines cofounded *Youth Advocates for Climate Action Philippines* (YACAP) in 2019 to protect the environment and amplify the voices of Indigenous leaders fighting for a green Philippines. Mitzi and her peers **organized school climate strikes** and galvanized a movement for change in their community.

Youth Strike 4 Climate activist, environmental educator, and climate podcaster Sophia Caralde organized an event where government officials engaged directly with the Youth Declaration, signaling progress toward climate justice and amplifying youth voices in shaping the direction of climate advocacy in the Philippines. The Youth Declaration is a document created by young climate activists that shows their goals for a better future and ensures their voices are heard in climate policy decisions.

Young leaders Keisha Mayuga and Jefferson Estela used different approaches and tools to fight for climate justice in the Philippines. An urban cyclist who grew up playing and biking in Manila's bustling city streets, Keisha introduced a biking activist project and worked with a sustainable transportation initiative aimed at tackling Manila's air pollution. Jefferson, on the other hand, led grassroots initiatives that addressed environmental challenges across the Philippines.

These actions, along with many others by young Filipino activists—from tree-planting campaigns and coastal clean-up drives to advocating for local financial institutions to withdraw their investments from coal companies and contribute to the transition toward renewable energy— have made a significant impact on the climate movement.

The Youth Climate Justice Movement in the Philippines continues to unify youth from different backgrounds in a collective pursuit of environmental justice. Their collaborative efforts still garner widespread recognition, capturing the attention of local and international media and inspiring others to get involved.

JUSTICE FOR GEORGE FLOYD

On May 25, 2020, *George Floyd*, a Black man, was killed by Minneapolis police officer *Derek Chauvin*, <u>sparking global outrage.</u> Floyd's arrest came after a shop worker reported a $20 bill he used to buy cigarettes might be fake. Chauvin, along with four other officers, detained Floyd, with Chauvin **pressing his knee onto Floyd's neck and back** for a harrowing 9 minutes and 29 seconds, **causing Floyd's death**.

Seventeen-year-old Darnella Frazier from Minneapolis recorded Floyd's arrest and death on her phone and shared the video online. It quickly went viral, leading to **widespread protests** and *"Black Lives Matter"* demonstrations worldwide. People united to demand justice for Floyd and an end to police violence and racism on and offline. Floyd's last words, **"I can't breathe,"** became a **powerful call to action** against police brutality and racism, emphasizing the urgent **need for change and accountability**.

Students and youth across the United States **joined in solidarity**, organizing and <u>demanding action</u> to end racial injustice and police brutality. Among them, 17-year-old *Tiana Day* led a **significant peaceful protest** in Northern California that attracted over 50,000 participants. This event was part of a larger movement, **showcasing the strength of youth activism in creating change**.

> People united to demand justice for Floyd and an end to police violence.

Young activists like Tiana were crucial in holding policymakers accountable and pushing for change. Their efforts helped bring Chauvin to trial, where he was eventually convicted and sentenced to more than 20 years in jail. The **public outcry also led to legislative action**, with over a dozen states **banning police chokeholds** after Floyd's murder.

Six-year-old *Gianna Floyd*, George Floyd's daughter, also **captured the world's attention**. In a video shared by her late father's close friend, Gianna, sitting on the friend's shoulders, declared,

> "Daddy changed the world!"

Her powerful statement highlights George Floyd's ongoing legacy and **the fight for justice and equality**.

MALAYSIAN YOUTH PUSH FOR REFORM

COVID-19 was spiking in July 2021, and the Malaysian people were **unhappy with their government's leadership** during the pandemic. To demonstrate their

> **BACKDOOR GOVERNMENT: OUT!**

discontent, they started <u>hanging black flags</u> from their cars and homes. The flags also appeared on social media profiles coupled with **#lawan**, which means "fight" in Malay, as a show of disagreement with the Malaysian government. One young black-flag supporter marked their protest on an urban street with a bold handwritten sign saying, "Backdoor Government: Out!"

> **WE STAND FOR THOSE WHO CANNOT**

The mostly peaceful youth-led "Black Flag" movement was born as 40 youth groups united under the banner of *Sekretariat Solidariti Rakyat* (SSR), or the *Secretariat Solidarity Party*.

Qyira Yusri, a young cofounder of #Undi18—an organization that **lobbied for lowering the minimum voting age** from 21 to 18 to increase <u>youth political participation</u> and advance equality—was a visible figure during the campaign. Youth activists were **tired of the government's delay** in allowing 18-year-old citizens to vote, despite Parliament's agreement in 2019.

With reports of over 20,000 daily new cases of COVID-19 by July 31, 2021, many protestors **demanded the ousting** of *Prime Minister Muhyiddin Yassin* and his cabinet. Some sat on the street, while others carried signs that said, **"Democracy by discussion, not oppression"** and **"We stand for those who cannot."** The protestors were unified in their concern about the country's leadership and banded together, with some focusing on other issues such as soaring unemployment, stuck wages, corruption, and rising housing costs. Black flags continued to be **displayed as a symbol of protest.**

Although the **authorities detained 47 protestors**, the demonstration continued. And arrests didn't just happen on the day of the action. Two days before July 31, *Sarah Irdina,* the 20-year-old founder of *MISI: Solidariti,* a youth-driven activist collective, was arrested for claims of sedition and held for tweeting about the upcoming protest. Since some **participants in earlier actions** had also been investigated, SSR used crowdfunding to pay Sarah's fine and worked with the *Young Lawyers Movement* (YLM) to ensure activists could access free legal support. Today, Sarah continues to **fight for social justice and political reform** after speaking up about experiencing harsh conditions in a small jail cell without privacy,

After the July 31 protest, Prime Minister Yassin stepped down, **inspiring Malaysian youth to organize** for racial justice, climate justice, education reform, and more.

COVID-19 STUDENT WALKOUTS

In January 2022, a few years into the *COVID-19 pandemic*, the highly contagious Omicron variant was on the rise. Students nationwide joined forces with teachers' unions and other activists to **protest attending in-person classes** in sometimes overcrowded and under-resourced schools. Some students left their classrooms, while others protested from home due to **insufficient support and screening for the virus**.

"SAFER SCHOOLS"

These student-led movements—from New York, where daily new cases in the city topped 50,000, to Illinois and Michigan—advocated for **safe learning environments** and **remote or hybrid classrooms**. Feeling unheard by local mayors and school board officials, students **took to the streets, social media, and news outlets** to raise public health concerns, build solidarity across borders, and raise awareness about the **impact of reopening schools on their health and safety**.

Frustrated by being **left out of decisions about their lives** and health, many students marched with handwritten signs demanding **"safer schools,"** used text messages and social media to spread petitions, and coordinated further walkouts for better conditions. Organizers also drew attention to the **educational disruption caused by studying in unsafe environments**.

> Students took to the streets, social media, and news outlets to ... raise awareness about the impact of reopening schools.

In Oakland, California, students vowed to return to in-person school only if improvements were made. In New York City, youth organizers called for a period of online lessons to help students **take responsibility for their health and well-being** during the pandemic. Disabled students and allies also voiced their frustration about choosing between their education and **the risk of exposing themselves or their vulnerable family members to harm**.

The COVID-19 walkouts were a **masterclass in the unifying power of online and offline storytelling and connection**. The stories young activists shared through social media posts and press releases were picked up by the media, inspiring students in other states to join the protests for public health and safety in schools. Each local movement was unique, but they all aimed to **ensure students were heard** and their well-being protected, on their terms.

WOMEN, LIFE, FREEDOM!

Mahsa Amini, a 22-year-old Iranian woman, was tragically killed in September 2022 after being arrested by Iran's morality police for **wearing her hijab headscarf in a way they deemed improper**. Witnesses reported that she was beaten in the police van, leading to her collapse when she reached the police station. It reportedly took half an hour for an ambulance to arrive and another 90 minutes to transport her to the hospital, where she remained in a coma for two days. Despite police claims that she died of a heart attack, **relatives and detainees cited torture and abuse during her arrest**.

> The slogan became a rallying cry against oppression and a beacon of hope for millions worldwide.

Journalist Niloofar Hamedi shared a photo on Twitter of Mahsa's distressed family holding each other in the hospital, **drawing attention to her case**. Mahsa died later that day in the intensive care unit, igniting a **firestorm of outrage** and sparking the global **"Women, Life, Freedom"** movement.

The movement, rooted in the **Kurdish struggle for autonomy and equality**, embraced the slogan "Woman, Life, Freedom," initially used by <u>Kurdish women activists</u>. *The Kurds*, an ethnic group with a distinct culture and language, have long sought freedom and equality due to historical **oppression and denial of their rights** in Iraq, Turkey, Syria, and Iran.

The slogan became a **rallying cry against oppression** and a <u>beacon of hope</u> for millions worldwide. As protests erupted in response to Mahsa's death, it echoed through the streets of Iran and beyond, with demonstrators **challenging the clerical**

leadership's authority and demanding the downfall of the *Islamic Republic* that was established in 1979. Clerical leadership means that religious leaders have a lot of power and make important decisions for the country. They decide on rules and laws based on their beliefs and understanding of religious codes.

Despite **government crackdowns** resulting in numerous arrests, injuries, and deaths of protestors, defiant acts were captured on social media, such as teenage girls in Tehran **cutting their hair**, removing their headscarves, chanting anti-government slogans, and dancing in public spaces. In specific regions of Iran, including Lorestan and Kurdistan, women have a history of cutting their hair in mourning. They **assert their independence and collective grief by cutting their hair**, especially when the government and religious leaders claim authority over their bodies. During the "Women, Life, Freedom" movement, **this act became a powerful protest, reclaiming the right to self-governance**.

Protestors posted footage featuring the violent backlash against them and cruelty by Iranian security forces with the message, **"Please be our voice."** They asked the world to **keep their stories alive** when they could not, due to forced lockdowns and having their access to technology and media blocked by authorities. The deaths of young activists in Iran, including 16-year-old protester *Nika Shakarami,* fueled <u>public outrage</u> as the movement gained momentum, with international solidarity seen in **rallies held worldwide** and support from unions, and human rights, student, and feminist groups.

"Please be our voice."

A year after Mahsa's death, thousands marched in her memory worldwide. Despite <u>ongoing suppression</u> in Iran, her legacy endures in the commitment of activists and the continued fight for gender justice.

A song, **"Baraye,"** by *Shervin Hajipour* remains an anthem for the movement, having reaching millions before Shervin was arrested and imprisoned for **"inciting people to disturb national security."** The song is one of the movement's most far-reaching artistic symbols, along with murals, posters, protest art, and poetry, all of which captured the spirit of defiance and solidarity that **define the continued battle for freedom of speech and expression in Iran.**

STUDENTS AGAINST BOOK BANNING

"We knew we were part of something bigger than ourselves, and we were part of the greater good."

These are the words of *Christina Ellis*, one of a group of young leaders from *Central York High School* in Pennsylvania who **successfully overturned** a book ban in their school district.

Between 2022 and 2023, book bans increased nationwide. In the first eight months of 2023, the *American Library Association* recorded 695 attempts to censor library materials, affecting over 1,900 titles. At Central York High School, the ban included **books by Black authors, people of color, Indigenous authors, and LGBTQIA+ authors**, and on essential topics such as civil rights and historical injustices. One of these books was *Young, Gifted and Black*, written for young people by me, the author of the book you're reading right now.

Christina Ellis, along with fellow students *Edha Gupta* and *Olivia Pituch*, recognized the **importance of engaging with** different perspectives in books to foster understanding and empathy. They led protests at school board meetings and faced criticism from their local community. Despite the challenges, the **number of students protesting kept rising**, and they persisted in their cause. Over time, their efforts led the board to reverse the ban. By protesting, the young activists reclaimed their right to access materials that would inform their thinking, and celebrated the value of inclusive education.

The protests **gained national recognition** through a *TEDx* talk delivered by Christina and Edha. This raised awareness and fueled a youth activism movement **against book censorship** across the United States. Young activists like 16-year-old *Iris Mogul* from Miami, Florida, created a banned-book club as a form of resistance. Seniors *Ella Scott* in Austin and *Da'Taeveyon Daniels* in Euless, Texas, were also prompted to launch banned-book clubs and join advocacy groups to combat censorship.

The efforts of students like Christina, Edha, Olivia, Iris, Ella, and Da'Taeveyon—along with others from Utah, Virginia, Tennessee, Georgia, Oklahoma, West Virginia, Florida, and more—highlight the **power of youth activism in protecting the right to read, learn, and express thoughts freely**. Young people continue to challenge censorship, shaping the future of education and safeguarding a more inclusive future by demanding their right to read

YOUTH PAVING THE PATH FOR PEACE

In 1967, *Muhammad Ali*, the 25-year-old heavyweight boxing champion, <u>made a historic stand</u> for nonviolence and the pursuit of peace. Amid the Civil Rights Movement and the Vietnam War, Ali refused conscription, stating,

> **"Why should they ask me to put on a uniform and go 10,000 miles from home and drop bombs and bullets on Brown people in Vietnam while so-called Negro people in Louisville are treated like dogs?"**

Because he stood up for his belief in peace, Ali was arrested, stripped of his heavyweight title, and banned from his sport for three years. Still, decades later, young people in countries with obligatory conscription—including Thailand, Ukraine, and Turkey—<u>are being detained</u> for refusing military service. In recent years, *Yeo Zheng Ye* from Singapore, *Tal Mitnick* from Israel, and *Song In-ho* from South Korea made headlines for their decision, joining a tradition of refusers whose beliefs have led to them enduring jail time, economic consequences, and social shaming.

Nonviolence and the pursuit of peace are ideals championed by youth beyond the issue of conscription. When the Israel-Gaza war began in 2023, high school students *Rawda Elbatrawish* and *Liora Pelavin*, from Teaneck, New Jersey, organized discussion sessions to **bring their Muslim and Jewish communities together** and foster empathy. *Dissenters,* a US student anti-war group formed to connect violence against Black and brown people to larger systems of global conflict, organized rallies, sit-ins, and online training to protest the Israel-Gaza war. And, as students at *George Washington University* and the *University of California* organized actions to demand the return of kidnapped Israeli hostages, student activists worldwide simultaneously called for an end to the humanitarian crisis in Gaza. It was at these campus protests that a piece of **protest art** from 1966 resurfaced—the iconic image of a sunflower by *Lorraine Schneider*, with the words

"War Is Not Healthy For Children And Other Living Things."

The tradition of **peaceful direct action** began in the 6th century BCE with the Jain community's emphasis on nonviolence and the teachings of *Gautama Buddha*. This ancient practice set the stage for leaders like *Mahatma Gandhi, Dr. Martin Luther King Jr.,* and *Muhammad Ali* to champion nonviolent resistance in their fight for justice. Standing up for humanity never gets old, and even if our approaches and visions vary, **the drive to make a difference and serve our communities, values, and conscience unites us all.**

FIGHTING FOR THE FUTURE

You met my mother at the beginning of this story. In honor of the way she lived, I'm going to give *Mama*, the person who introduced me to *John Lewis* and his motto **"Get in Good Trouble,"** the last word. (She would not have it any other way.) Mama is going to take us off these pages and out into the world.

Early on, Mom used to say, **"No one is coming to save us, so we need to save ourselves,"** when other adults at dinner parties would try to kick tweenage me out of political discussions and back to the kids' table. Mom would slyly wink approval when others would try to shoo me away and remind me of my place outside of being seen and heard—but **I have learned the value of standing in my truth with a tall backbone and a strong, open heart** if I have something important to say.

I always wanted to sit at the table with the people who could vote—so I could influence them. If I disagreed with someone, I liked to **listen to understand their motivations** as I discerned my own beliefs. I didn't know it then, but I had a knack for strategy and influencing the officials who made decisions that impacted me, and it still comes in handy today.

I return to this memory as each day unfolds with grim reminders of the ongoing suffering endured by communities worldwide, amid a landscape of **crisis, war, economic injustice, and inequality**. As an American who spent her formative years abroad, I've experienced firsthand how connected we all are, no matter where we live. It's a reminder that **we cannot afford to be bystanders**, watching injustice and doing nothing, but rather catalysts for change, bearers of hope, and creative architects of a greater tomorrow—made better when we **work together and embrace our empathy** to achieve this.

The echoes of history **resound with the voices** of those who dared to challenge the status quo, confront injustice, and envision a more just and equitable world. One voice I didn't mention in the book but has been in my ear throughout its development stands out. *Anne Frank*—eternally 15 years old—whose words pierce through time with a timeless urgency:

"How wonderful it is that nobody needs to wait a single moment before starting to improve the world."

Anne's story is a **testament to the power of resilience, defiance, and hope**. Despite the darkness that enveloped her world, she **refused to be silenced**, penning her truth and shaping the course of history with her words. Her legacy reminds us that even in the darkest times, our voices can ignite change and illuminate paths to a brighter future.

But it isn't just about looking to the past for inspiration; it's about finding our own voice, paths, and ways to make a difference. It's about recognizing that **each of us has a role in the ongoing struggle for justice, equality, and liberation**. Whether it's through joining grassroots movements, volunteering to help others in need, speaking out against injustice, making influential art with a message, or advocating for change, there are **countless avenues for young people to make their mark on the world**.

At the time of this publication, there are over 100 armed conflicts plaguing the world, with women, children, disabled people, poor people, and other vulnerable populations bearing the brunt of the effects of violence, hunger, and abuses of power.

We have a lot of work to do to transform what needs healing and fixing, and history has shown us that those most closely affected know the roots of what is required. We, and the rest of the world, must listen to and amplify those voices—an important step we can all take that **costs nothing but our courage and our hearts**.

Let's be guided by the belief that <u>our collective efforts,</u> no matter how small, can ripple outward and shape history. As the young people in this book showed us, **there is another way, even if we can't see it yet**, that we can envision the change, long before we see it blossom into its fullest power.

Your stories matter, no matter where you live or how old you are. I believe in you, your power, and the role people of all ages can play in shaping a future where none of us are left behind or on the sidelines. Looking back on my journey from the young person who was shooed away and still took a stand to the woman I am today, I admire and respect the leadership of next-generation voices in authoring the next chapter in human history.

So, I ask you: how will you remake the world? Your voice, actions, passion, and commitment to justice are needed now more than ever. Let us **unite in solidarity and determination** to build a world that is truly worthy of all who inhabit it on a planet deserving of our full respect, attention, and love.

YOU'VE GOT THIS, BECAUSE, AS ALWAYS, WE'VE GOT US.

KEY DAYS OF ACTION AND COMMEMORATION

JANUARY 1
New Year's Day
Emancipation Proclamation Day

JANUARY 15
Dr. Martin Luther King Jr.'s birthday
(annually observed on the third Monday in January)

JANUARY 27
International Holocaust Remembrance Day

FEBRUARY 4
World Cancer Day

FEBRUARY 20
World Day of Social Justice

FEBRUARY 21
John Lewis's Birthday (US)

MARCH (first Thursday)
World Book Day (UK & Ireland)

MARCH 8
International Women's Day

MARCH 22
World Water Day

MARCH 25
International Day of Remembrance of the
Victims of Slavery and the Transatlantic Slave Trade

APRIL 7
World Health Day

APRIL 22
Earth Day

APRIL 23
World Book Day (rest of the world)

MAY 1
International Workers' Day or International Labor Day

MAY 3
World Press Freedom Day

MAY 15
International Day of Families

MAY 25
Africa Day

MAY 28
World Hunger Day

JUNE 5
World Environment Day

JUNE 12
World Day Against Child Labor

JUNE 16
Youth Day (South Africa)

JUNE 19
Juneteenth (US)

JUNE 20
World Refugee Day

JUNE 21
National Indigenous Peoples Day (Canada)

JUNE 26
International Day in Support of Victims of Torture

JULY 2
Anniversary of the 1964 Civil Rights Act (US)

JULY 11
World Population Day

JULY 12
Malala Yousafzai's Birthday (World Malala Day)

JULY 30
World Day Against Trafficking in Persons

AUGUST 9
International Day of the World's Indigenous Peoples

AUGUST 12
International Youth Day

AUGUST 19
World Humanitarian Day

AUGUST 26
Women's Equality Day (US)

AUGUST 28
Anniversary of March on
Washington for Jobs and Freedom
Anniversary of Dr. Martin Luther King Jr.'s "I Have a Dream"
Speech (US)

SEPTEMBER 5
International Day of Charity

SEPTEMBER 8
International Literacy Day

SEPTEMBER 21
International Day of Peace

SEPTEMBER 30
National Day for Truth and Reconciliation

OCTOBER 11
International Day of the Girl Child

OCTOBER 16
World Food Day

OCTOBER (second Monday)
Indigenous Peoples' Day (US)

OCTOBER 24
United Nations Day and the beginning of Disarmament Week

NOVEMBER 20
World Children's Day

DECEMBER 1
World AIDS Day

DECEMBER 10
Anniversary of the Adoption
of the Universal Declaration
of Human Rights

PEOPLE HAVE POWER!

GLOSSARY

Annulment (election)
Annulment of an election means declaring it invalid because of cheating or unfairness that makes the results unreliable.

Apartheid
A system of racial segregation and discrimination.

Authoritarianism
A political system characterized by centralized power, limited political freedoms, and often suppression of dissent through control of media.

Autonomy
Independence and the ability to make decisions without external control.

Colonialism
When a powerful country takes control of another place, exploiting its resources, enforcing its laws, and often imposing its own culture on the existing population.

Colored
Colored people in South Africa, historically labeled under apartheid for their mixed ancestry, have a unique language combining Afrikaans, English, and Indigenous languages like isiXhosa and isiZulu, that reflects their diverse Cape Colony heritage.

After apartheid, many people of African, Asian, and European descent embraced the term "Colored" to proudly reclaim their mixed-race identity, fostering unity in a society moving towards inclusivity. Some people identify as both Colored and Black, blending different cultural backgrounds that contribute to the country's richly diverse identity.

Communism
An economic, political, and cultural system where the government and the community controls and manages all of the resources and how they are distributed to people. It is supposed to mean equal distribution of wealth in a classless society, but it can have an impact on personal freedom, and economic and cultural growth. Communism can be practiced in many different ways, and current communist countries include China, Cuba, Laos and the Democratic People's Republic of Korea.

Concentration camp
Sites of mass detention and suffering, with detainees held there based on their identity or beliefs. Concentration camps were historically used during times of conflict or persecution.

Congressional Gold Medal
A prestigious award honoring people for exceptional achievements that benefit society, granted by the US government.

Conscription
A practice by which people are forcibly enlisted into military service, often during national emergencies.

Death penalty
The death penalty, also called a "death sentence" or "capital punishment," is when a government or state executes someone who has been found guilty of committing a serious crime. Crimes that can be punished with the death penalty are called capital crimes or capital offenses. While over 50 countries still allow the practice, over 100 countries have abolished it.

Draft (military)
The selection for military service based on specific criteria and reflecting national policies during times of conflict.

Federal
A word that refers to national governance encompassing all states and territories. Federal laws and policies affect the entire country.

Get-out-the-vote campaign (GOTV campaign)
A well-planned direct-action campaign or mission that teaches people about voting, helps them register, and motivates them to cast their ballot. A GOTV uses different ways to connect and engage more people in the democratic process.

Grassroots
A word that describes movements that mobilize ordinary people to advocate for social change from the ground up, often outside of traditional political structures.

Guerrilla fighter
An unconventional fighter using surprise tactics against stronger adversaries, often for political or social change.

Humanitarian
Someone who is committed to promoting human welfare and alleviating suffering, guided by compassion, empathy, justice, and solidarity.

Imperialist
Someone who believes in extending their country's power and influence over other countries, often by taking control of them and exploiting their resources.

Intersectionality
A term used to recognize how interconnected identities such as race, gender, and class shape individual experiences, societal structures, and access to resources and privileges.

LGBTQIA+
An inclusive term for diverse sexual orientations and gender identities that advocates for equal rights and acceptance.

National Guard
The reserve military force in the United States, mobilized during emergencies and supporting community needs.

Pardon
Official forgiveness for a crime, granted by a government authority.

Racial profiling
The practice of targeting individuals based on their race or ethnicity when a crime is suspected, contributing to systemic injustice and discrimination.

Referendum
A direct vote by citizens on a specific issue or law, influencing public policy and decision-making.

Socialist
Someone who supports socialism—a system and an ideal that advocates for collective ownership and control of resources to promote social equality and reduce economic disparities.

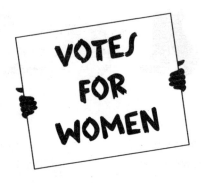

Suffragist
Someone who fights for suffrage—the right to vote—for people who are unjustly kept from voting and having fair participation in the electoral process. Suffragists throughout history—including women suffragists who chose to be known as "suffragettes"—have fought to change laws and beliefs that prevent certain groups of people from being able to access and cast their ballot.

Unconstitutional

Refers to laws or actions that violate principles and rights outlined in a constitution. Anything unconstitutional is against those rules.

Union

A group of workers who come together to organize for their rights, benefits, wages, and working conditions.

Wildcat strike

An action taken by workers—without union approval—to stop working to demand better conditions or pay. It's like taking a timeout during a game to ask for fairer rules.

FURTHER READING

A Bigger Picture
by Vanessa Nakate

Fight Back
by A. M. Dassu

Good Night Stories for Rebel Girls
by Elena Favilli and Francesca Cavallo

How Women Won the Vote
by Susan Campbell Bartoletti

I Am Not a Number
by Jenny Kay Dupuis and Kathy Kacer,
illustrated by Gillian Newland

Jamie
by L. D. Lapinski

Kid Activists: True Tales of Childhood from Champions of Change
by Robin Stevenson, illustrated by Allison Steinfeld

Kid Authors: True Tales of Childhood from Famous Writers
by David Stabler, illustrated by Doogie Horner

Marley Dias Gets It Done: And So Can You!
by Marley Dias

No One Is Too Small to Make a Difference
by Greta Thunberg

Rad American History A-Z: Movements and Moments That Demonstrate the Power of the People
by Kate Schatz, illustrated by Miriam Klein Stahl

Refugee
by Alan Gratz

Resist
by Veronica Chambers

Streetcar to Justice
by Amy Hill Hearth

The Hate U Give
by Angie Thomas

This Book Is Feminist
by Jamia Wilson, illustrated by Aurélia Durand

We Rise, We Resist, We Raise Our Voices
edited by Wade Hudson and Cheryl Willis Hudson

Who Was Rosa Parks?
by Yona Zeldis McDonough,
illustrated by Stephen Marchesi

ABOUT THE AUTHOR AND ILLUSTRATORS

Jamia Wilson is an award-winning feminist activist, writer, speaker, and podcaster. Wilson has contributed to *The New York Times*, *The Today Show*, CNN, BBC, Oprah Daily, *Teen Vogue*, *Elle*, the *Guardian*, and more. She is an author of books for all ages, including *Young, Gifted and Black*, *Step Into Your Power*, *Big Ideas for Young Thinkers*, and more. She is also a co-author of *Road Map for Revolutionaries* and the introduction and oral history to *Together We Rise: Behind the Scenes at the Protest Heard Around the World*. **www.jamiawilson.org**

Photo by Aubrie Pick

Devon Blow is a multitalented artist from Los Angeles, California, specializing in illustration, design, writing, and social justice activism. Her work passionately advocates for marginalized communities while celebrating cultural diversity. Notable clients include The Obama Foundation, Oprah's Book Club, The *LA Times*, and the United Nations.
www.devthepineapple.com

Ashley Lukashevsky is a Queer Mixed-Asian artist originally from Honolulu, Hawaii. Ash uses illustration and visual art as a tool to strengthen social movements for our collective liberation—racial justice, immigrant justice, climate justice, mental health, and LGBTQIA+ liberation. They believe that we need to be able to envision a world beyond harmful systems, and that art can be a pathway to do just that.
www.ashleylukashevsky.com

Photo by Rey Robles

ACKNOWLEDGMENTS

To WFW aka Dr. Mom—to eternity and beyond you are always here, breath by breath and step by step. Thank you for inspiring me to keep writing always.

To JRW aka Daddy—thank you for sharing your passion for writing and books.

To TOS aka Trav—thank you for the soundtrack for this book from Chopin to free jazz.

Thank you to the phenomenal DK team: Katy, Tori, Emma, Anne, and Jon. I am forever grateful for your vision and leadership. Thank you to Ashley and Devon for your creative brilliance and powerful storytelling.

To James Baldwin, thank you for this reminder and call to action to make love "a popular movement":

"The world is held together ... by the love and the passion of a very few people. Otherwise, of course, you can despair. Walk down the street of any city, any afternoon, and look around you. What you've got to remember is what you're looking at is also you. Everyone you're looking at is also you. You could be that person."

(James Baldwin)

Find your voice and own the room, so you can speak up with confidence!

Be inspired to use your power, no matter how big or small, to support others.

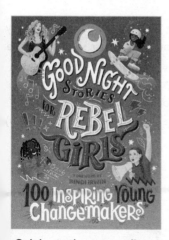

Celebrate the extraordinary young women who are making their mark on the world today.

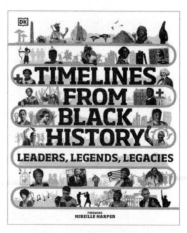

Delve into the unique, inspiring, and world-changing history of Black people.

Senior Editor **Tori Kosara**
Project Art Editor **Jon Hall**
Senior Acquisitions Editor **Katy Flint**
Managing Art Editor **Vicky Short**
Production Editor **Marc Staples**
Senior Production Controller **Louise Minihane**
Art Director **Charlotte Coulais**
Managing Director **Mark Searle**

Written by **Jamia Wilson**
Jacket art by **Ashley Lukashevsky**
Interior illustrations by **Devon Blow**
Edited for DK by **Emma Roberts**
Designed for DK by **Anne Sharples**

DK would like to thank Megan Douglass and Shari Last for
proofreading, Dee Hudson for the authenticity review,
Phil Hunt for fact checking, and Jessica K. Taft for
her contribution as a consultant.